The Key to Your Man's Heart

Dr. H. NORMAN WRIGHT

Regal

From Gospel Light
Ventura, California, U.S.A.

PUBLISHED BY REGAL BOOKS
FROM GOSPEL LIGHT
VENTURA, CALIFORNIA, U.S.A.
Regal PRINTED IN THE U.S.A.

Regal Books is a ministry of Gospel Light, a Christian publisher dedicated to serving the local church. We believe God's vision for Gospel Light is to provide church leaders with biblical, user-friendly materials that will help them evangelize, disciple and minister to children, youth and families.

It is our prayer that this Regal book will help you discover biblical truth for your own life and help you meet the needs of others. May God richly bless you.

For a free catalog of resources from Regal Books/Gospel Light, please call your Christian supplier or contact us at 1-800-4-GOSPEL or www.regalbooks.com.

Edited by Amy Spence

Library of Congress Cataloging-in-Publication Data

Wright, H. Norman.
  The key to your man's heart / H. Norman Wright.
     p. cm.
  Includes bibliographical references.
  ISBN 0-8307-3334-5
  1. Wives—Religious life. 2. Husbands—Psychology. 3. Marriage—Religious aspects—Christianity. 4. Christian women—Religious life. 5. Christian men—Psychology. 6. Man-woman relationships—Religious aspects—Christianity. I. Title.
  BV4528.15.W75 2004
  248.8'435—dc22   2003027465

1 2 3 4 5 6 7 8 9 10 11 12 13 14 15 / 10 09 08 07 06 05 04

Rights for publishing this book in other languages are contracted by Gospel Light Worldwide, the international nonprofit ministry of Gospel Light. Gospel Light Worldwide also provides publishing and technical assistance to international publishers dedicated to producing Sunday School and Vacation Bible School curricula and books in the languages of the world. For additional information, visit www.gospellightworldwide.org; write to Gospel Light Worldwide, P.O. Box 3875, Ventura, CA 93006; or send an e-mail to info@gospellightworldwide.org.

Contents

CHAPTER 1

Key to Your Man's Heart

Who *is* that special man in your life? How would you describe him to someone else? Go ahead. Give it a try. What words come to mind? Does he know how you would describe him? If not, why not? Sometimes we can get so busy in a relationship that we end up living parallel lives and never really connect. That's what this book is about: connecting by understanding the uniqueness of the special man in your life and learning new ways of relating to him. It may involve learning new ways of communicating with him. Some women have said, "I'd just like to communicate in *any* way with my man!" You may have a quality relationship with your man and just want to step it up a notch, or you may be frustrated and discouraged and wonder if anything can be done. There is something that can be done.

UNDERSTANDABLE DIFFERENCES

What do you know about the man in your life? What do you understand about him? The phrase, "I just don't understand that man," is one of the most frequent statements of all statements that you hear from women. You can understand your

Men are not that complex, unusual or weird—they're just different.

special man. Men are not that complex, unusual or weird—they're just different. Their bodies are different and their minds are different. They think and experience life differently from women. Some differences happen genetically and some are culturally determined. How are men different from women?

Just for openers:

- Men snore more
- They fight more

- They change their minds more often than women do
- Their blood is redder
- Their daylight vision is superior
- They have thicker skins and longer vocal cords
- Their metabolic rate is higher
- More of them are left-handed
- They feel pain less than women
- They age earlier (unfortunately)
- They wrinkle later
- Rich men are fatter than rich women
- Men's immunity against disease is weaker
- Men talk about themselves less
- They worry about themselves more
- They are not as sensitive to others as women are[1]

Men are constructed differently inside and out. Have you ever heard women complain about men and weight loss? "It isn't fair! Why can my husband lose weight easier than I can? I work and work at it and it's a struggle, but it seems to be easier for him and other men." It's sad but true. Men have an easier time losing weight than women do. Why? Because men's fat is distributed differently from women's. Men lack the layer of fat just underneath their skin that women have. They also have more muscle than women: 41 percent compared to 35 percent. The greater proportion of muscle to fat makes it easier for men to burn fat. One of the sad facts of life!

Some men like to be thought of as male machines. These men are a special breed different from women, children and other men who don't measure up. The male machine is functional and designed mainly for work. He is programmed in a special way to tackle jobs, attack problems, override obstacles, overcome challenges and, above all, always take the offensive side. If any task is presented to him in a competitive manner, he will take it on. Winning and achieving is all the reinforcement he needs. He has relationships with other men built upon respect rather than close, intimate friendship. Intimate relationships are an enigma to him.

Does he sound familiar in part or whole? This describes some men and perhaps reflects a stereotype that is an unfair label. Even though men differ from women, they also differ among themselves.

MIXED MESSAGES

Our society creates confusion within a man because of the mixed and numerous messages he hears about being a man. Society's expectations for men are often in conflict, as are his own expectations for himself.

Society's expectations for men are often in conflict, as are his own expectations for himself.

He is supposed to be "all male" and yet be "a sensitive man." He struggles with being the strong, silent lone wolf versus being one of the guys; being the family man versus being independent and always in control; being a handyman versus being helpless.

As a man develops, he is confronted with his own personal expectations that he has developed from many sources. Yet these may not match up to who he is. A man's roles in life—such as husband, father, son, friend, elder, deacon, professional—carry certain expectations, and there may be conflicts between some of these roles. All men have expectations of what they would like to be, but they also find inconsistencies between these expectations and what they are actually becoming.

Consider the conflicts expressed in this description:

Men are raised to take charge,
  but they cannot all be their own bosses.
Men are raised to be the primary providers,
  but they find they are now living during inflation
  and recession.
Men are raised to focus on achievement,
  but success is usually a momentary experience.
Men are raised to stand on their own,
  but they need support systems.
Men are raised to express "strong emotions,"
  but they often feel "weak" ones like fear and
  sadness, too.
Men are raised to be team players,
  but it's often "every man for himself."
Men are raised to be Daddy's Big Boy,
  but expect to remain Mommy's Little Man.
Men are raised to be independent,
  but urged to bond and nest.
Men are raised to follow their dreams,
  but required to be realistic about security.[2]

HEART MATTERS

The focus of this book is to describe men in order to understand them. Some women have asked, "Are all men this way or am I just crazy?" I hope that you will gain greater insights concerning men in general and the men in your life specifically. This isn't a book to let men off the hook from their roles and responsibilities in relationships, but it is to assist women. I believe that a man is responsible for the temperature of a relationship. Biblically, he is to take the lead—especially in spiritual matters—and he is to understand his wife (see 1 Pet. 3:7) and love her as

There is hope— increasing your understanding of your man, learning new ways of responding and praying can accomplish more than you realize.

Christ loved the Church (see Eph. 5:25-33). He is to model a servant's attitude. There is no reason today for men not to learn and know how to respond in this way. Helpful resources are abundant. Seminars are constantly being offered to help men upgrade their skills and calling.

Yes, it is true. Some men need more help than others. Unfortunately, some women feel stuck in their relationship—

there's no hope that anything will ever change no matter what they do. But there is hope—increasing your understanding of your man, learning new ways of responding and praying can accomplish more than you realize.

If you would like to understand and relate to men—and allow them to be who they are to their fullest potential—ask yourself these questions:

1. What are my beliefs and stereotypes about men?
2. Do my beliefs and stereotypes limit me in allowing men to be different and unique?
3. Do I respond to men in a way that perpetuates behavior on their part, which reinforces my view of them?
4. Do I respond in any way that limits my growth and development as a woman?
5. Do I in any way reinforce men's tendencies to use work as their source of identity?
6. If the man in my life has a relationship type or work style that bothers me, do I in any way tend to reinforce that style?
7. In any way do I suppress my own identity, assertiveness or sexuality in my relationship with my man?
8. Am I willing to upset the balance and equilibrium in a relationship with a man and create a crisis in order to bring about positive change? Growth does not usually occur for a man without some crisis to create introspection and progress.
9. Do I make it clear in my relationships with men that it is safe for them to be open and honest about their feelings with me?
10. Am I disconnected from the influence of men in my

past so that I am free to develop in my relationship at this time?

Consider these questions by yourself and then discuss them with other women. See what you can learn about yourself (this is one step in understanding a man).

Some of what you will read in this book has been written before in a few of my other books such as *What Men Want* (Regal Books, 1996), *How to Encourage the Man in Your Life* (Word Publishing, 1998) and *Understanding the Man in Your Life* (Word Publishing, 1987). It has been repackaged and simplified so that you will receive the heart of the material.

INNER STRUGGLES

Women have written numerous books and articles explaining their confusion about and lack of understanding of men. Rarely, however, do men speak out in response to what women don't understand about them. I asked men point-blank: "What is it that you think women *do not* really understand about men?" and "What are men's greatest inner struggles?" I received responses from more than 200 men on a multiquestioned survey given in various settings. Their responses to these questions were similar, and perhaps the best way to begin is to listen to one man who was appointed spokesperson to share the thoughts of many men. This is what he had to share:

What I am going to share with you are not my own thoughts and beliefs, but those that have come from the hearts, the minds and the lips of concerned men. They wished to remain anonymous and we will honor their privacy. They have a dual message to share. They wish to be heard and understood by women, and they also want to encourage other men to speak out.

Allow their words to touch your hearts as these men speak for all of us. As much as possible, their own words and phrases are used. Here is what they said:

> We believe women don't fully understand that men are different from women. They appear to realize that they are different from us, but they don't understand how different we are from them—and that it is good that we are different. The difference is not a negative. Let's keep in mind that God created us differently for a purpose. And it is good. We don't want to be like women.

> We know women want us to understand them. We are trying. But please cut us some slack and understand us, too; don't think all men are alike. We aren't.

> We men are competitive. We like it. We enjoy it. We also like "blazing new trails" and conquering new things like our ancestors did when they hammered out the new frontier during the founding of our country.

> Some of us go too far in this tendency [of competitiveness] and must be reminded of the need for balance. Keep in mind, however, that our competitiveness is needed to succeed for our

families. Women often have difficulty accepting our "hunter" instincts. They don't understand our drive to win the race, accomplish the goal or complete the task. Sometimes we have a need to appear macho or masculine or whatever you wish to call it. We want to appear strong and in charge of ourselves, to others, especially other men. Is this wrong?

Our inner struggles are caused by our whole quests for balance. We strive to find a balance between "fighting for providing, hunting and succeeding" and "being sensitive, caring, approachable and loving." These two concepts seem opposed. The world tells us to be tough, strong and in control; yet we want to be sensitive, available and nurturing.

We also struggle with the balance between work and family. Family life takes time. Work life takes time. Both demand a lot of energy, sacrifice and determination. Both require personal resources. We men are stretched to the limit. We need to replenish our energies—our physical energies, mental energies and spiritual energies. Yet we struggle because we want to give 110 percent in every area of our lives.

Women don't usually enjoy the same hobbies and interests that we do, but we want them to know that we need these outlets. They help us to *forget work*. And we need to forget at times. When we play with the women in our lives, often we just want to play—not talk.

We need to feel important. Whether it's work, sports, hobbies or family, we are searching for significance, approval and success. We have different drives and motivations, but most women don't recognize this. Our drive for success is often camouflaged with phrases like, "It's no big deal"—but it is a big deal. And it is a very big deal to look good around our peers.

One man was quite candid with his thoughts about this subject:

Most women know about men's egos, but they see our egos as character flaws. They fail to see that our egos can also be interpreted as positive qualities. Our egos compel us to lead, to serve and to protect women. We need to be valued and respected as family leaders and protectors.

Most men are creators—builders. It can be anything from hot rods to barbecues to room additions. We enjoy serving women in this way, but women need to explain what they want before we complete the project. It is disheartening and unmotivating to have to make changes once the job is finished. We hate to hear, "Oh, I wish we had done this instead" after the work is done.

Most women don't understand that maturity is more than facial hair. We want women to be patient with us as we develop into men. We need guidance, mentoring and male friendships to grow and mature.

We struggle with establishing identities. We can build relationships and we need male fellowship. But we define ourselves by what we do, not by our friendships. We want to know: Is this wrong? Is this a problem?

We long to be appreciated for "who we are," especially at home. We want to experience unconditional love at home—not just performance-based love. We struggle with that all day long on the job. When we come home, we don't always want to hear how hard our wives have worked. We need to hear some loving compliments, not just complaints!

Do women really understand how we feel about the responsibility for making ends meet? Their actions tell us they don't. We feel burdened to provide for the family whether our wives are employed or not. Many of us fear disappointing the family and failing in our roles of protector, provider, father, family leader and spiritual head. Our self-worth, our ego and our identity are linked to both work and home. It often appears that we are not as interested in what goes on at home as we are with what happens at work. That may not always be the case— we just may be exhausted from work. It is frustrating for us not to have more time to give of ourselves at home.

One man expressed his greatest inner struggle this way:

It is really tough being a man—at least the man that God expects me to be. There is a lot of internal pressure if I truly want to be a man of God—a leader in my home; a good, tender, loving and understanding husband; a gentle, wise, available and compassionate dad; a model and diligent worker (employee); and a trustworthy, listening

and responsible friend. These are just a few of the responsibilities of a godly man in addition to being truly and
wholly committed to loving, serving and obeying God.

Another man shared his struggle:

I struggle to live up to not only life's but also my wife's
various expectations—you know, job position and success, good father, perfect husband. But actually, my
greatest struggle is overcoming the past without missing
the now and destroying the future. For example, I labor
with not letting my nonfeeling past rob me of feeling
today. My grief over missed opportunities often destroys
today's joy and tomorrow's possibilities. I feel like the
weaker vessel, and at times, I can barely handle the flood
of emotion myself, let alone share it with another—especially a woman. Lord knows how she will react and use it
against me. But I am working on it, regardless of the
consequences.

Another man said:

We need to feel needed and know we are important at
home. We are sensitive to not only *what* you say but also
how you say it. Criticism shuts us down. We want our
wives who are full-time homemakers and haven't worked
in the competitive, chaotic work world outside of the
home to understand that it is difficult and challenging
for Christian men to interact and work under the con-
stant influence of non-Christian attitudes all day.

One man summed it up for most men when he said:

We men live in fear of losing our income and our health, and of our mortality. Our energies are spent keeping up our image of being good men and successful providers.

Then we come to the big issue we're always taking hits about—emotions, feelings or whatever you call them. There is confusion here for both men and women. We are emotional beings. We are not as insensitive as we are stereotyped to be, but we have difficulty moving from the logical/linear side of the mind to the emotional—that is, if we are left-brained males. Not all of us are left-brained either.

We do need to be emotionally connected to the women in our lives. Women tend to label us as loners. It's not true for all of us—alone at times, yes, but not loners.

LITTLE-KNOWN FEELINGS

There are a couple of reasons why men keep their deep feelings to themselves: (1) men want to spare and shelter their wives from pain, and (2) men fear they will be told what to do or be interrogated about what they have shared.

It is painful to be referred to as "typical males" and to always hear how incomplete and inadequate we are. We need to be accepted and appreciated for the way God created us.

Read what three men said about feelings:

I would say many women don't understand the reality and depth of emotional pain men feel, especially when it relates to feelings of inadequacy imposed by society's markings of a real man—financial success, sexual potency, physical stature, competency and so on. I wonder if the average wife knows how much her husband needs her support, admiration and affirmation.

My wife says things to me that hurt deeply. She says them in passing without much emotion or anger, just off the cuff. She seems to say them at times when discussion would be inappropriate (e.g., when other people are present). When we finally do get time to talk, the hurt is less severe or I just let it pass. This is probably more my problem than hers.

We struggle with emotions and stress. It seems that women, even those from the feminist groups, feel that they have all the stress. I don't know if they understand the gigantic responsibility we face being God's umbrella of protection of our families in a world that has such great negative influence and unhealthy attractions. It is hard to keep all your ducks in a straight line at times.

Perhaps you relate to these three men. Perhaps you are bothered by what they have said. They're not alone. They're a voice for men: past, present and future. Let me continue with some more responses from men:

We need an abundance of emotional encouragement, positive strokes, touching and compliments, just as women do. Those of us who are high achievers often mask our intense fears of failure and inferiority with our successes. We just don't like to admit it.

Some of us feel crippled. Many of us won't ever fulfill the expectations of our wives. Can't we work out some level of compromise?

Many of us would like to communicate with our wives, as intimately as they communicate with their friends. But we find it difficult. Who will help us learn? We receive few offers—only complaints.

Women say we are single-minded. We are. Single-mindedness helps us reach our goals. We have difficulty listening when we are concentrating on something else. We are accused of being purposely inattentive and made to feel guilty and even attacked for this. Why?

We want women to understand that we need more time to process what is said to us than women do. When we feel pressured to be different, we may use anger as our protection—to get others to back off.

Stereotypes limit us. Women are convinced that all men think about is power and sex, or sex and power! So when we do open up emotionally, our response is automatically classified to one of these areas.

Women believe that all we think about is sex. Well, yes and no. Sex is on our minds a lot. We are constantly barraged with sexual temptation in the media—from newspaper ads to films. They hit us at our weakest point. The guy who says he never notices is either lying or a walking cadaver.

Our eyes are the problem. Men have innate visual scanners for anything sexually appealing. Don't think we don't notice. The old adage "Women have to be in the mood, and men have to be in the room" is true. Resistance is a struggle for Christian men.

There is also a strong connection between a man's sex drive and his ego. Women need to know how they impact us. The way they dress, wiggle, look or touch us affects us. We constantly struggle with keeping our sex lives pure, especially when our wives are cold. Sometimes we don't want to be romantic—we just want to do it. Other times we need to know we are desired, loved and accepted. We enjoy having our wives take the initiative.

One man stated the problem of male sexuality well:

I don't think women fully understand our sexual struggles, because they just don't think the same. It's like trying to explain back pain to someone who has never had it. Something gets lost in the translation.

Here is another man's response to the questions we asked:

We want women to know that although we are often too nonverbal and unemotional, we do care. We get the message that if we really loved our wives, we'd adapt to their ways. Perhaps there is some truth in that.

DISCUSSION

Here are eight statements from men that may leave you with some material for thought and discussion:

1. Men are not personal saviors. We cannot be the perfect fathers you had hoped for when you were growing up. Too much is expected of us by women. We want you to receive more from the Lord, so you will need less from us.

2. Men are the heads of the households, and we need our wife's support with raising children. This concept is not a threat to the women's authority—it supports it.

3. I feel that women are out to change us. We need to work together and allow our differences to complement each other.

4. I think women judge us for not processing the way they do. We tend to judge women for the same reason. Each wants the other to be more like themselves; therefore, we are both left with unfulfilled expectations.

5. My greatest struggle is understanding women. They are so complex. Just when I think I have a handle on the situation and I think I see a ray of hope in understanding my wife's feelings, she throws another log on the fire, which makes me feel hopeless. There are times when I feel like giving up and getting a divorce. But I don't believe in that! Then I feel maybe it's me, that I am super stupid. Yet when I see other men having the same problems, I realize I am not stupid (ignorant maybe, but not stupid). Anyway, I keep praying for God's wisdom.

6. Most men change when women respond to them with love and tenderness (i.e., gentleness—not loud or defensive behavior). Deep down men want intimacy—they just have not learned how to achieve it. Men need to be loved.

7. I believe there is very little women don't really understand about men. I feel rather transparent with my wife. I will even welcome her counsel.

An attorney who has practiced family law for several years summed up his thoughts after counseling thousands of men:

8. After interviewing numerous men struggling with their marriages, there seemed to be a fairly common pattern about what men think women do not understand about them. The most common answers are the need for time apart, relaxation, male bonding, sports development and physical needs.

Now that you've read these men's honest responses, let's summarize the various points you have read regarding men's inner struggles and feelings on life's expectations. Write down a key point about men in each space provided.

1.

2.

3.

4.

5.

6.

7.

8.

9.

10.

11.

12.

13.

14.

15.

Now go back and indicate which of these reflects the man in your life.

Have you discussed any of your thoughts with him? If so, what was his response?

What were your feelings as you heard his response?

Knowing this information, how will it assist you in connecting with your special man in a different way?

This isn't everything you need to understand about men. There's more to come.

CHAPTER 2

Don't Blame Him —It's His Brain!

Then God said, "Let us make man in our image, in our likeness, and let them rule over the fish of the sea and the birds of the air, over the livestock, over all the earth, and over all the creatures that move along the ground." So God created man in his own image, in the image of God he created him; male and female he created them.

GENESIS 1:26-27

That's where it started. In the Garden of Eden, God created male and female. And He created each in a unique way. He made male and female *very* different, more than most realize. And what He made *so* different you can't see. Let's consider a very special difference—the brain. (Yes, all men have brains.) An adult brain weighs about eight pounds. It has three layers of dense matter and each layer has specific functions. Each brain has as

God made male and female *very* different, more than most realize. And what He made *so* different you can't see.

many cells as there are stars in the Milky Way (100 billion neurons) and has 100 trillion connecting cells. Can you fathom that amount?

You may be thinking, *How does a man's brain differ from a woman's brain?* A boy's brain matures later than a girl's brain. For example, girls acquire their complex verbal skills as much as a year earlier than boys. Often preschool girls read faster, have a larger vocabulary and have better grammar. Right from the beginning, boys start out with a communication deficit and disadvantage. And this continues into adulthood. Sometimes women expect men to be on an equal basis verbally. But how can they be?

Girls take in more sensory information than boys. Girls tend to hear better, see better and simply take in more information through their fingertips and skin. When a woman tells a man, "How can you not get it? It was so obvious," to him it wasn't. If you expect your man to be equal to you with his verbal abilities and quickness in verbal responses, it may not happen.

Girls generally tend to have better verbal abilities, so it's easy for them to rely on what works best—verbal communication. But if that isn't developed as much, what might you rely more on? That's right, nonverbal communication. Boys tend to rely more on this. You see, most men are not as quick in their abilities to verbalize feelings and responses as women. Therefore, expecting a man just to come out with his response quickly and extensively is an unrealistic expectation. If you put pressure on a man, you may not only get the opposite of what you want, but you're also likely to be the recipient of his anger.[1]

THE BRAIN AT WORK

Let me give a basic course in biology, physiology and anthropology. If you have read this information in other books, this may be a good review. However, for many of you, this information may be very new.

Consider how the brain functions—yours and his.

Left Side

The left hemisphere controls language and reading skills. It gathers information and processes it logically in a step-by-step fashion. When is the brain's left side used? When you read a book or article, play a game, sing, write, balance your checkbook and weigh the advantages and disadvantages of buying an item on time versus paying cash.

If you're planning your day's schedule, you may decide to leave 10 minutes early to drop off the video you rented the night before, and you'll plan the route that will enable you to park in front of the store. How did you make these decisions? By using the left portion of your brain. It keeps your life sensible, organized and on schedule. It's like a computer.

Right Side
Then there is the right side of the brain. That portion of the brain comes into play when you work a jigsaw puzzle, look at a road map, design a new office, plan a room arrangement, solve a geometrical problem or listen to musical selections on the stereo. The right half of your brain does not process information step-by-step like the left portion. Instead, it processes patterns of information. It plays host to your emotions. It has been called the intuitive side of the brain. It links facts together and comes up with a concept. It looks at the whole situation and, as if by magic, the solution appears.

Left Side Versus Right Side
The thinking pattern of the left side of your brain is analytical, linear, explicit, sequential, verbal, concrete, rational and goal oriented. The right side is spontaneous, intuitive, emotional, nonverbal, visual, artistic, holistic and spatial.

If you are more right-side oriented and your man is left-side oriented, how will you communicate? It's as though you speak different languages! And you probably do!

Have you ever been in a class or even a church service where the speaker focused on dry, detailed facts? If the person was inflexible, he or she was probably annoyed by interruptions to his or her train of thought, so after each distraction the individual *would return to the beginning* and review. The step-by-step speech was most likely monotonous with little emotional expression. If this scenario sounds familiar, you were probably listening to a person who was an extreme—and I mean extreme—left-brain-dominant person.

The Brain

Analytical		Spontaneous
Linear	**L R**	Intuitive
Explicit		Emotional
		(women excel)
Sequential		Nonverbal
Verbal		
Concrete		Visual, artistic
Rational		(women stronger)
		Spatial
		(men stronger)
Goal oriented		Holistic

If you listen to a speaker or someone in a conversation who rambles from topic to topic, relies on his or her own opinions and feelings, is easily led away from the point, leaves gaps in the presentation to give the conclusion and uses emotional language and hunches, you're in the presence of an extreme right-brain-dominant person. The left side wants to know, "What's the bottom line?" while the right side travels around the barn a few times to get there. As you'll see later, personality differences will affect how a person responds.

When you were in school, you probably ran into individuals who excelled in math or reading but flunked playground! Why? They were functioning with a highly advanced left brain, and the right brain was less developed.

Ask yourself, *If a man who is a highly proficient chemist also enjoys social activities and dancing twice a week, which portion of his brain is he using for these tasks?* He is using the left side for his work, which must be careful, accurate and logical. When he's out dancing, he feels the steps by shifting to the right side of his brain. The chemist may be more comfortable using his left side, but he's able to make a switch for some right-brain activities. We shift back and forth between these two sides of the brain as we carry on our daily activities.

Remember, we will constantly reinforce our dominant side because it's easier to go that route than to break new ground by using the less dominant side.

If your man is left-brain dominant and you are right-brain dominant, here are some common *right-brain-dominant* complaints about a *left-brain-dominant* man. As you read these complaints, indicate with a check mark whether or not this reflects your man.

You feel your man is	Yes	No
Emotionally unavailable to you	___	___
Preoccupied when you're together—even obsessive	___	___
Not in the here and now—always in the past or future	___	___
Too inhibited—can't let go and play	___	___
Insensitive—too blunt in what he says	___	___
Self-centered and even antisocial	___	___
Distant—you don't feel needed by him	___	___
Closed and won't talk about feelings	___	___
Not romantic in the way you want— doesn't merge emotionally during lovemaking	___	___
Not demonstrating a caring attitude toward you in a way that connects	___	___
Boring in conversation, too factual—doesn't like to chat	___	___
Too invested in routine and isn't flexible	___	___

If you are left-brain dominant and your man is right-brain dominant, you may complain in this manner:

- He gets too emotional when he talks about problems.
- He wants too much of my companionship.
- He draws attention to himself.
- He won't stay on one topic.
- He does not take a logical approach to problem solving.
- He personalizes things; he is too sensitive.
- He doesn't have enough interests; he needs to be entertained.
- He jumps to conclusions about my behavior.
- He isn't direct about his wants and needs, and expects me to "know" his wants and needs; he places too much emphasis on becoming "one."
- He doesn't appreciate and devalues the ways I demonstrate my caring.
- He shares too many irrelevancies in conversation.
- He doesn't pay enough attention to details; he is careless.

All of us have *some* of these characteristics because we operate from both sides of our brain.[2]

BRAIN DIFFERENCES BETWEEN MEN AND WOMEN

Allow me to go back in time and look at the brain differences in boys and girls. Assume you have X-ray glasses that allow you to look into their brains. As you look inside, you may see a discrepancy between boys and girls.

In the brain there is a section that connects the left and right hemispheres. It's a bundle of nerves (the technical name is corpus callosum), and there are up to 40 percent more of these nerve bundles in girls than in boys. This means that women are able to use both sides of their brains. In other words, women use their brains holistically.

This extra connective tissue in girls is a reason why they develop language skills earlier than boys and use many more words than boys do. Do you know why boys often don't read as

A man's brain has been geared to develop his spatial skills, which is why throughout his life he wants *to do* something about everything.

well as girls? It's the brain again. *The brain that reads better is the brain that uses both sides of the brain at once.* Interestingly, it's also easier to "read" the emotions on a person's face when you use both sides of your brain simultaneously.

A woman's brain has been developed to express and to verbalize. This is why throughout adulthood she wants *to talk* about everything. A man's brain has been geared to develop his spatial skills. This is why throughout his life he wants *to do* something about everything. Essentially, a woman is usually quicker to talk about her feelings, while a man wants to act quickly to do something about them. Has this been an issue for you?

Of course, you recognize this is where the conflicts arise (and probably always will). A woman will say, "Let's sit down and talk this through." Meanwhile, the man is straining at the bit to get the problem fixed and get on with life. Remember, neither response is wrong, and neither is better than the other.

In studies at the University of Pennsylvania, brain-scan equipment has been used to generate computer photographs of brains in use. They look almost like maps. The equipment produces pictures of the brain in different colors, each color showing a different degree of intense cortical activity.

To get this mapping, a man and woman are hooked up to the equipment and both are asked to do a spatial task—to figure out how two objects fit together. If you looked at a computer screen depicting a woman's brain, you would see that the color and intensity on both sides are fairly equal. Something else happens in the man's brain: The right side lights up with various colors that reflect a high degree of right-brain activity and much less left-brain activity. But if verbal skills are tested, watch out! The man uses much less of his brain compared with the woman's use of her brain. Her left hemisphere really lights up.

In a recent seminar, I had the opportunity to see such pictures. A woman's brain scan showed activity on both sides of the brain when she was talking. When the man was talking, the brain scan indicated activity only on the left side of his brain.

The findings of this research indicate that a woman's brain is at work almost all the time in more sections than a man's brain. It's as if both hemispheres are always on call; whereas, in a man's brain, one hemisphere at a time is on call.

Think of it like this: If there's a task to do, a man's brain turns on. When the task is completed, the brain turns off. That's a simplified version. Yet a woman's brain is always on. It's true that parts of a man's brain are always on, but when the two brains are compared in their downtime—or inactive time—the difference between the portion of the woman's brain that is always on and a man's brain that manifests an on/off function is quite pronounced.[3]

Other results prove the fact that women have 40 percent more, and thicker, nerve connectors between the two sides of the brain.

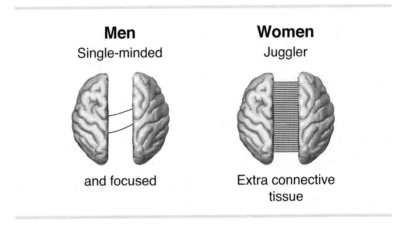

Men
Single-minded

Women
Juggler

and focused

Extra connective
tissue

Perception and Intuition

Women can tune into everything going on around them. A wife may handle five hectic activities at one time while her husband is reading a magazine, totally oblivious to the various problems going on right under his nose. She can juggle more often but can be distracted more easily. He can focus on one task more effectively but can lose sight of other aspects. He has to stop one activity in order to attend to another. (Have you ever expected your man to handle several things at one time?)

The result of this difference: Women are more perceptive than men about people. Women have a greater ability to pick up feelings and sense the difference between what people say and what they mean. Women's intuition has a physical basis. A woman's brain is like a computer that can integrate reason and intuition. This intuition drives some men crazy. There are numerous stories about couples who have gone out socially and the wife says to her husband, "I think there's a problem or something is going on." Her husband responds with, "How do you know? Where are the facts?" She replies, "I don't have any facts. I just sense it." He says, "You don't know what you're talking about." But a week later, when he finds out she was right, he's amazed and even more puzzled. Bill and Pam Farrel describe this scenario in their clever book *Men Are Like Waffles—Women Are Like Spaghetti:*

> In contrast to men's waffle-like approach, women process life more like a plate of pasta. If you look at a plate of spaghetti, you notice that there are lots of individual noodles that all touch one another. If you attempted to follow one noodle around the plate, you would intersect a lot of other noodles, and you might even switch to another noodle seamlessly. That is how women face life. Every thought and issue is connected to every other thought and issue in some way. Life is much more of a process for women than it is for men.
>
> This is why women are typically better at multitasking than men.
>
> Men are like waffles, women are like spaghetti. At first this may seem silly, even juvenile, but stay with us. It is a picture that works and men "get it" because it involves food.
>
> What we mean is that men process life in boxes. If you look down at a waffle, you see a collection of boxes separated by walls. The boxes are all separate from each

other and make convenient holding places. That is typically how a man processes life. Our thinking is divided up into boxes that have room for one issue and one issue only. The first issue of life goes in the first box, the second goes in the second box, and so on. The typical man lives in one box at a time and one box only. When a man is at work, he is at work. When he is in the garage tinkering around, he is in the garage tinkering. When he is watching TV, he is simply watching TV. That is why he looks as though he is in a trance and can ignore everything else going on around him. Social scientists call this "compartmentalizing"—that is, putting life and responsibilities into different compartments.

One of the characteristics that creates havoc in male/female interaction is the fact that most men have boxes in their waffle that have no words. There are thoughts in these boxes about the past, their work, and pleasant experiences, but these thoughts do not turn into words. A man is able to be quite happy in these wordless boxes because the memories he carries in them have significant meaning to him. The problem is that he cannot communicate these experiences to others, and so his wife may feel left out.

Not all of the wordless boxes have thoughts, however. There are actually boxes in the average man's waffle that contain no words and no thoughts. These boxes are just as blank as a white sheet of paper. They are EMPTY! To help relieve stress in his life, he will "park" in these boxes to relax. Amazingly, his wife always seems to notice when he is in park. She observes his blank look and the relaxed posture he has taken on the couch. She assumes this is a good time to talk as he is so relaxed, and so she invariably asks, "What are you thinking, sweetheart?"

Ladies, when it is your husband's turn to talk, you need to practice staying in the box he wants to open. You see, when he brings up an issue for discussion, he actually intends to talk about that issue. So when he says to you, "We need to talk about our finances," he most likely wants to have a financial conversation. If he says he wants to talk about your upcoming vacation, he probably wants to talk about your vacation, and so on. He is hoping this time will be different. He wants to have what he considers to be a reasonable conversation with you. He wants it to stay on track. He wants to identify the problem, evaluate the options, commit to a solution, and see it work out.

A problem develops because you immediately recognize all the issues that are related to the one thing he brought up. It is as if you can see every box that is touching the box he has opened. You feel the need to open all those boxes because they are relevant to the discussion. If you don't open them, you are afraid the loose ends will never be addressed. You know that it has backfired in the past, but you haven't ever really understood why, so you try again.[4]

Senses

It could be that women pick up more information than men do since their senses such as hearing, eyesight, taste and smell are more heightened than men's senses.

The hearing difference is noted even in childhood. Men, in general, hear better in one ear. Females, in general, hear equally as well in both ears and hear more data than men. Throughout a lifetime, males hear less than females say, which creates profound problems in relationships.

It's been noted that boys from very early on ignore voices—even parents' voices—more than girls do. Why? In some cases boys are simply not hearing. They also do less well at picking out background noises than girls. Boys, quite simply, hear less background noise and differentiate less among various sounds. This is one of the reasons why parents and anyone around a boy often report having to speak louder to a boy than to a girl.[5]

What does this difference mean? It is the main reason why men are fixers—task oriented—and not as able to do several things at once. They need to focus on one thing at a time. When a man takes on a task at home such as cleaning the garage or working in the yard, to him it's a single-focus task, *not a fellowship time.* If his wife wants to work with him, she usually wants to carry on a conversation at the same time. To him this may seem like an interruption—an invasion of his space, a distraction—and he may react strongly to it. Millions and perhaps billions of conflicts over the years could have been avoided if men and women had not only understood this difference but also honored it.

A woman's multitask approach, as opposed to a man's single-task approach, tends to make a woman feel that her man isn't listening. He is listening, but he just may not be ready. A wife complains, "It's obvious. Why can't you see it?" He can't see it because that's not the way he thinks.

A husband says, "Just take one step at a time—you can't approach it that way." But she can. Neither the man's nor the woman's approach is wrong; they're just different. Can you imagine what a couple could accomplish if they learned to use each other's creativity and strength?[6]

Problem Solving
Generally speaking, when it comes to approaching and solving problems, women use both sides of the brain and are able to cre-

ate an overview. Men tend to break down the problem into pieces in order to reach a solution. They use a linear approach by going through steps 1, 2, 3 and 4. Women tend to go through steps 1, 3, 2 and 4 in order to reach the same conclusion. If a woman arrives at the same conclusion before her man does, he probably won't accept her answer as correct, because he hasn't completed steps 1, 2, 3 and 4 yet. He's not ready for her answer.

Order

Men like structure. Men like to put things in order. They like to regulate, organize, enumerate (men love to talk about numbers and statistics) and fit things into rules and patterns. It's not unusual for men to take the time to put their CDs and videos in alphabetical order or to figure out how long it will take to walk 2 miles or drive 85 miles to their favorite fishing hole.

Ever wonder why some men have a set routine on Saturdays? Maybe the order is wash the car, mow the lawn, trim the roses and take a nap. And it's always done at the same time in the same order.[7] Order provides structure and conserves energy. Keep the word "energy" in mind, for it's the source of contention between men and women.

EXCLUSIVE VERSUS INCLUSIVE

The way in which men use their brain is an exclusive mode. (Some women refer to it as tunnel vision!) This mode can cause men to exclude everything except what they are focusing on. It shuts out other possibilities. And men exert an abundance of energy to stay in this position. Most men like to know exactly where they are and what they are doing at any given point in time. It's a way to stay in control.

When a husband is at home and his attention is locked on the TV or newspaper or on fixing the car, he's in his exclusive mind-set. If his wife talks to him, he feels an interference or intrusion. *And for him it's an energy leak.* He hopes it will leave. When he exerts energy to shift from whatever he is doing to concentrate on his wife, he becomes upset because of the energy expenditure. He has to change his focus and shift it elsewhere, because he can't handle both at once. She feels he's inconsiderate for not listening, and he feels she's inconsiderate because of the intrusion. Actually, neither is inconsiderate. They just don't understand the gender difference. If they did, each person could learn to respond differently.

A woman sees and responds to life like a camera with a wide-angle lens, whereas a man's camera has a highly-focused microscope lens.

Women are inclusive and can jump in and out of different topics. There's no energy drain for them. A woman actually picks up energy by entering into new experiences or changes. She is able to see the situation and beyond. She sees and responds to life like a camera with a wide-angle lens, whereas her man's camera has a highly-focused microscope lens. He sees the tree in great detail; she sees the tree, but she also sees the grove and its potential. A woman's expectation of a man's perceptual ability should be tempered with this knowledge.[8] Bill and Pam Farrel describe exclusion versus inclusion in their own words:

> In conversation she can link together theological, emotional, relational and spiritual aspects of the issue. The links come to her naturally so the conversation is effortless for her. If she is able to connect all the issues together, the answer to the question at hand bubbles to the surface and is readily accepted.
>
> This often creates significant stress for couples because while she is making all the connections, he is frantically jumping boxes trying to keep up with the conversation. The man's eyes are rolling back in his head while a tidal wave of information is swallowing him up. When she is done, she feels better and he is overwhelmed. The conversation might look something like this:

> > Joan gets home and says, "Honey, how was your day? I had a good day today. We just committed to a new educational wing at the university, so I have been asked to oversee the budget. I am so excited that they didn't rule me out because I'm a woman. You know women have been fighting for a place in society for decades, and it is good to see so much progress being made. I think it is neat that you treat the women who work for you with so much respect. Our daughter is so lucky to have you for a dad. Did you remember that Susie has a soccer game tonight? I think it is important we are there because the Johnsons

are going to be there, and I really want you to meet them. Susie and Bethany are getting to be good friends, and I think we should get to know her parents as well."

As Joan is exploring this conversation, Dan is getting lost. He has no idea what the budget at the university has to do with their daughter's soccer game and their need to have a friendship with the Johnsons. He admires her ability to connect seemingly unrelated thoughts but he just can't seem to understand how she does it.[9]

Remember, there will be exceptions to what is said here. Some men and women will be just the opposite. My wife and I are exceptions. I tend to be the juggler and she is more single-minded. It also appears that personality preference has a modifying effect on some of these characteristics.

Here's another issue: Since a man usually focuses on one thing at a time and a woman can handle several things at one time, if she's multitasking while talking to him, he feels she's not paying attention to him. If she were interested, she would look at him with 100-percent attention. Does this scenario sound familiar?

Yes, the differences are there. And yes, there's good reason for the differences. Here's a question to consider: How will you respond to the man in your life in a different way? It may help to describe what you will do in writing.

CHAPTER 3

What Men Don't
(or Won't) Talk About

Years ago I conducted two major surveys to discover what men are reluctant to discuss. The first survey was sent to more than 700 professional counselors, ministers, lay counselors and social workers. The survey question was What are the five most frequent questions or issues that men ask in counseling? I was amazed to receive more than 700 responses.

Included in those 700 responses were more than 3,500 questions that men ask. Each question was carefully considered, and only the most frequently asked questions were selected for this book.

The issues raised by some men who sought counseling revealed a sense of desperation. Their many attempts to resolve their problems resulted in a futile dead end. They realized they needed help. Other counselees sought help during the early stages of their concerns before reaching the desperation stage. Depending on where you are in your relational development, you may find yourself identifying with some of these questions as well as the questions derived from our second survey.

The second survey was a self-report presented in numerous conference settings and churches throughout the country. Four questions were asked:

1. What subject(s) do you think men hesitate most in bringing up or discussing with women?
2. What is it that you think women do not really understand about men?
3. What is the greatest inner struggle that men deal with, which women either do not know about or understand?
4. What one thing would you like your wife to do that would indicate to you that she understands and accepts what you deal with in your daily life?

The men were asked to give detailed responses; however, even with the anonymity of the survey, many men were reluctant to complete the forms. The responses that did come in, however, were invaluable. The men who responded represented all ages from various churches throughout the nation.

What you are reading in this book is a reflection of many men, not just the author. Many men opened up and responded in ways that their wives wished their husbands would respond to them.

CATEGORY 1: EMOTIONS

The first category of responses to question 1—What subject(s) do you think men hesitate most in bringing up or discussing with women?—focused on projects, the past, change, appreciation, personal relationships, conflict, vulnerability (i.e., weakness or insecurity) and what women want. The answers were repeated consistently by those who responded. The following responses are gleaned from the second survey:

> I don't think most men like discussing subjects that add onto their "Honey Do" lists. We feel busy enough. I watch the excontractor neighbor walk away briskly as we all stand in the street talking about our house projects, when his wife changes the subject to her wish for a remodeled kitchen! I know I turn off the switch in my head when I have "her" list, because I'd rather be tinkering on my projects. That's honest. I also don't think men like to hear or see commercials about the gals' period time of the month. We freak out. If a woman talks about this in serious terms, we don't know or want to know the details.

> Deep personal feelings that perhaps we ourselves are afraid of or don't understand.

> Job issues or other problems where we've had a "history" of issues, for example, having a hard time keeping a job.

> Concerns or issues that never were dealt with or solved with our own mothers that now come up in various ways in our marriages. For example, how can I give to

someone else emotionally when I never received emotional support? How can I explain this?

Change. In general it is difficult to discuss changing certain aspects of our lives because of the uncertainty the changes might bring or require. I know that sounds like a lack of faith, but I also know that the Lord has put us where we are for a reason and that He has given us the ability to make decisions and process things.

Attempted projects that are failing; negative financial situations; details about people and events.

The need to be appreciated.

Deep needs or insecurities, inadequacies and temptations.

The wife's feelings about the state of her relationship and where it needs improvement.

I think the subjects men most hesitate to bring up with women are sex and finances. Because they provoke such personal feelings and attitudes, they are very sensitive subjects. Both men and women have such innate differences of approach to each of these subjects that conflict is very probable, and the possibility of conflict makes men hesitate in bringing up the subjects. If we were attentive to discussing these and other difficult subjects when things were good in these areas and not just at times when things were bad, maybe it wouldn't be so difficult to discuss them with women.

Personal relationships. I do not like to pry into the personal relationships of others. When a conversation heads in this direction, I quickly resort to what God has to say—who can argue?

Potential conflict (this is different for each couple); insecurities or areas of perceived failure (i.e., problems at work, lack of spiritual growth or plateaus); things that make us different. In today's world, men experience pressure to conform to the way women want us to be.

Issues or sins from the past that cause fear because of embarrassment or rejection. For example: sexual behavior (i.e., pornography, homosexuality) and criminal acts (i.e., theft, assault). Lingering feelings regarding these things and persistent desires for them. Feelings about work.

If you talk about any other women, they had better be ugly. If the topic comes up my wife seems to want to compare, rate and know what I think and why.

In short, their own vulnerabilities. In our society men are supposed to be strong, self-sufficient, Clint Eastwood types. Men impose this on themselves. It is difficult for men to show weakness or vulnerability, especially to women.

Our weaknesses, struggles, sex, lust, relationships, finances, business loans and private schooling.

Weakness in two areas: character and discipline.

A man's reputation is important to him. When character issues come up, he translates them to be attacks on his reputation, when in reality he is dealing with an inner quality.

My wife and I share *everything* and are *very* open—we have a great marriage—and there is *only very slight hesitation* regarding the intimacy of our sex life. *Except* for the actual act, we never discuss sex, *but I suppose* it is *not* that important.

Any performance or character attribute that makes them feel less than perfect, especially their own sexuality and feelings or job-related inadequacy.

How they feel about being a man and how hard it is for men to open up to themselves much less to other men or to women. Women are too quick to tell men how they feel rather than helping them get in touch with themselves and their emotions.

Insecurity. They don't have it all together; they are not perfect; they need help; they need a woman to come alongside them and make life successful. This plays itself out in needing public affirmation, and it also plays itself out in needing sex. It may come across to women more like, "Hey, I need sex" than "I need you to know that I'm insecure in this area."

Their leadership roles in the family. In today's society the man's role is recognizable. We as Christian men are told what our roles are to be biblically. But when we take a stand, *sometimes* we are pegged as chauvinists—unfortunately, even from Christian women!

My answer would be twofold. First, my wife has experienced some abuse and does not feel open about our sexuality. In order to protect her, I have to approach how I feel very carefully. I don't want her to feel pressure, but at times she does. Second, my own moments of anger. When she is angry she expresses *herself freely*, but I tend to hold back. I would like more *freedom* to express my frustrations or anger.

True heartfelt problems. A woman's emotional makeup many times does not enable her to just *listen*. She starts talking and makes it worse.

Men hesitate to emotionally open up to their wives because of the uncertain outcome.

Men's expectations of "who" and "what" they want their wives to be. It is especially tough to discuss expectations when a man's wife is not meeting his expectations. It is even more difficult to discuss when the man doesn't even have a clear picture of those expectations himself. Sometimes I think my expectations are too high or unrealistic, so if I don't have a handle on them in my own mind, how can I discuss them with my wife?

The previous comments confirm that men hesitate to open up emotionally to their wives because of the uncertain outcome. They feel fear about potential conflict, discomfort about being personal, embarrassment, rejection, shame about admitting weakness, an inability to know how to respond and a concern about hurting their partners.

Each reason for being hesitant is legitimate; however, it is also insufficient to justify silence and prolong the lack of communication in relationships. The stressful residual effects of bottling up emotions can be enormous.

In response to question one, an attorney gave a summation of his experience with men:

Being able to nudge men into expressing the subjects they most hesitate to bring up or discuss with women is an almost impossible chore. It is tantamount to a confession that men find hard to share. I am an attorney, a certified legal specialist in family law, and in the 20 years I have been practicing, I have interviewed thousands of men who were experiencing marital problems, trying to ascertain what were their chief concerns. If I was lucky, I could barely get the men to identify *one* subject they hesitated most in discussing with women. Generating conversation was next to impossible, although it was clear that many subjects were of concern. I think the biggest problem is simply getting men to discuss any issues at all with women. Certainly some subjects men are less hesitant to bring up or discuss with women than others. I think these include finances, family budget, social activities, sports and, to a lesser extent, personal intimacy. If there is one category to define all the subjects that men hesitate to talk about, it would be in the area of emotions. Men do not like to discuss their hurts, stress, lack of accomplishment and questions related to their energy levels. All of these, of course, would fall under the general heading of the inability to express personal feelings.

CATEGORY 2: FINANCES, COMMUNICATION, FEELINGS

The second category of responses to question 1—What subject(s) do you think men hesitate most in bringing up or discussing with women?—centered on fears related to finances, communication and feelings. The following are the men's self-reported responses from the second survey:

Quality of fathering. Asking questions such as How am I doing as a husband? or How are we doing as a couple?

Men's fears—namely, financial and work-related. Also, men's abilities to be good fathers and husbands. Men also seem to question their relationship skills and appear hesitant to bring this up around women.

Financial problems and mistakes (i.e., a bounced check). Personal sexual desires and needs (i.e., different style or position for sex).

Masculine and feminine role issues. Men fear being accused of being sexist.

Discipline of children is a tough subject, because women have preconceived ideas that make it hard to act as priests of the home.

Finances, sex and things I would like to see my wife do (e.g., exercise and improve diet, dress better and other improvements related to house and home).

Finances, children, shortcomings and fears of succeeding, and not ultimately providing them with emotional support.

Getting older, reaching lifetime goals, mortality.

Fears. Attraction to other women. Pressure of supporting the family. Frustration of unfulfilled desires and dreams.

Finances is a tough subject because it usually leads to one of us coming across as accusing the other of unnecessary spending.

Finances in Detail

What questions and issues concern men most about finances? We referred to the first survey, which asked over 700 counselors to report the five most frequent questions or issues that men ask in counseling.

Questions from 40 categories were compiled. Finances were near the top of the list, ranking ninth in frequency. Can you identify with any of their questions?

- Can't she spend less on herself and the kids? Can't she work part-time and help with these bills?
- How can I advance my career and provide more money for my family?
- How can I be financially responsible and still do what I want?
- How can I deal with a wife whose spending is out of control?
- How can I tithe and pay all of the bills?
- How do I establish a budget?
- How do I get control of my spending and still give my family the things they need?
- How do I handle the problem of managing money when it is "her money" or "my money," not "our money"?
- I feel tremendous financial pressure. How can I cope?
- I may be unemployed soon. How do I support my family?
- My wife and I fight over finances—I want to pay the bills, she "needs" to buy stuff. What's the solution?
- My wife gets so frantic about money. How can I help her to grow in faith and stop worrying so much?

Communication in Detail

Another group of questions from the first survey reflects men's concerns about communication—with their wives and with others:

- Why do I have trouble showing and telling my family how I really feel?

- How do I communicate more effectively with my adolescent children?
- I can't open up to her. In my family we didn't show our feelings. What can I do?
- She won't hear me out, so I clam up.
- We keep going over the same ground. How many times do I have to reconquer the same territory?
- What should I say?
- When I choose to be honest about my feelings, why do I feel so weak and misunderstood?
- When I start sharing my feelings (i.e., fears and anger) it only triggers her feelings. Then I, in turn, stop sharing. I feel that there's no place for me to share my feelings.
- Why am I so afraid to tell others how I feel or what I need? Why don't I trust?
- How can I tell the truth when it might come back to haunt me?
- Why can't I communicate with women—or other men?
- Why can't she see where I'm coming from?
- Why can't we talk without things getting out of hand?
- Why do I have to tell her how I feel and ask for what I need?
- Why do women always want to talk?
- Why should I open up? (She'll just get mad if I tell her what I think the problem is.)

Feelings in Detail

Feelings and emotions, in addition to the man-woman relationship, pose endless struggles for men. Hear what men are saying about these topics, according to the first survey:

Personal fears and "perceived inadequacies." Any subject that triggers my wife's insecurities, resulting in hours of defensive discussion to alleviate her fears.

Men's feelings of insecurity, incompleteness, inadequacy, loss of control of family and situations, lack of self-confidence and relating to past mistakes. I personally did not want to share the above with my wife until this learning experience—I will share now!

Feelings and emotions, in addition to the man-woman relationship, pose endless struggles for men.

Feelings of inferiority, depression, anxieties and so on. Men see it as weakness, and I think we feel women will view it likewise. As Thoreau said, "Most men lead lives of quiet desperation."

It is very difficult for men to talk about sexual desires, personal feelings and emotions. I am very analytical. Black and white. On and off.

Their hidden fears of being rejected when dealing with *feelings* with spouse or friends. Sometimes it is hard to drop that "private wall" around those "feelings."

Emotions. Also, they won't talk a lot about family brokenness. They hesitate to speak of loneliness, sadness or pain. Many times the only thing that will break them loose is when the wife is ready to walk out.

Emotional, feeling-oriented issues. Also, issues dealing with failure, since culturally men are to be strong and in control.

For me, the subjects hardest to discuss with my wife are my fears and insecurities and my sense of inadequacy I often experience. Another subject that is difficult to discuss is my struggle with lust, though I think my difficulty in discussing it is also rooted in fear—fear of rejection, fear of hurting her, fear of facing my own corruption.

Men's spiritual relationships with God. Their shortcomings.

The inner struggle of juggling work, social life, family life and spiritual life. Knowing when and how to talk sensitively with my wife about my feelings and thoughts.

Anything that concerns a man's innermost thoughts and feelings. Two that come to mind right away are past failures (i.e., job, relationship and so on) and desires concerning sex and intimacy.

Fears of life: failure, inferiority, losing one's job, impotence.

We also referred to the first survey based upon the counseling responses to discover specific questions related to men's feelings:

- How can I get in touch with and express my feelings without feeling inferior or that I am not in control?
- How can I share my feelings and still maintain my masculinity?
- How do I deal with feelings that have been denied?
- If I gave up drinking, smoking and burying myself in work to let myself feel, could I handle it?
- Isn't it unreasonable for my wife to expect me to talk so much about emotions?
- Why am I so set on not expressing my emotions or showing my real emotions even though I'm hurting so much on the inside?
- Why do I numb out?
- Why is it so hard for me to talk about feelings or to cry?

With which questions do you identify? What would you add?

What surprises you about these questions? Are some of these statements reflective of the man in your life? What can you do to encourage more sharing? One man provides us with a possibility:

I'll tell you what would help me share more with my wife. For me to open up with her, there has to be no risk. I can be honest, but I don't want to be hassled. I don't want to be judged for what I share, and I want to share for as long as I want—and then have the freedom to quit when I need to.

That's it: No risk! No risk! Risk is a big factor in the man-woman relationship. Men are risk takers in many other areas of life but only in areas where they can fall back onto other resources. For men, sharing feelings presents a risk with a bottomless abyss waiting for them if they slip.

COMMUNICATION OBSTACLES

Other men have expressed what hinders them from sharing and what would help them:

> My wife is an expert on what is a "feeling" and what isn't a "feeling." I have tried to tell her what is going on inside of me and she tells me, "But that's not a feeling." Where is the book she uses to tell herself what is a feeling and what isn't? I feel like giving up if I'm never going to get it right.

> Yeah, I shared my feelings. And you know what happened? I opened up about work and my frustrations, and she claimed I just wanted sympathy and attention. I tried to show her some love and attention and she said, "You must want something, like sex. You've got some other motive in mind." I try to be what she wants, and I get criticized because my motives are suspect.

> My wife tells me what I ought to be feeling. If she feels a certain way, I should feel the same way. If we watch a gripping movie, she wants me to feel what she feels. When she cries at church, she says, "But didn't you feel the same way? How could you not feel that way about what was shared?" Women's feelings are not the only right feelings, and if I have to feel the same way, it will never work. Can't two people in the same situation feel differently with a different intensity—and even express it differently?

It is important first to define the issues clearly. I don't think women do this very well. They latch onto the first thing that comes to mind and get totally emotionally involved in it. The next thing you know, you are arguing about everything under the sun, and no one is happy. I believe in a clear definition of the problem at the outset. If she can tell me exactly what is bothering her, we can deal with it logically. If she can't do that, then there is no sense even talking about it.

Men are just more rational than women. We prefer to deal with things in a thoughtful, rational way. Women are emotional, and that's the way they want men to deal with things. Just because a man prefers to discuss things logically doesn't mean he is any less involved than a woman who wears her emotions on her sleeve.

I don't like responding to her question, "Is that what you *really* mean?" or her comment, "That doesn't make sense to me."

If I don't say I love her or I have missed her or I don't notice how she looks pretty in the right way, she gets upset. When I do express these feelings, she responds with, "Really?" or "Do you mean it?" I just hate that. She seems to be questioning my sincerity. Why can't she accept my words at face value?

That's just me. That's the way I am. She may not like it, but that's me. I'm quiet. I think (she hates to hear that word) most men are, and I wish women would accept this fact. Just because I don't share a lot with her doesn't mean I don't love her. I do love her. I just don't want to get into unending discussions.

Men have learned clever techniques for withholding their feelings. The message they send to the world is that emotional expression and survival don't mix—and they believe it!

Many men choke when it comes to sharing tender, caring feelings with others. They are not cruel, insensitive, noncaring people; they merely find it impossible to communicate their inner reservoirs of emotional expression.

The message they send to the world is that emotional expression and survival don't mix—and they believe it!

I have talked with such men. I remember one in particular who said, "I was so proud of my wife the other day. She has been taking some art lessons and finished her painting. It was displayed in the window of the artist's studio and two people wanted to buy it for an incredible amount of money! I don't know that much about art, but I thought it was great and was really feeling good about her success."

I replied, "That's great. How much of what you just shared with me did you tell her?"

He looked at me and said, "Well, I'm sure she knows how proud I am of her."

I replied, "How? How would she know that? Did you tell her what you told me? Did you tell her you were proud of her? Did you tell her you were feeling good about her success? Did you tell her you thought her art was great?"

He waited pensively, then looked up at me and said, "No, I guess I didn't. It would make a difference, wouldn't it?"

I replied, "Yes, it could change her perception of you to that of a caring person if you would let her in on those feelings."

COMMUNICATION AIDS

What is the best way for a woman to express her emotions to her husband—especially if he has difficulty coping with feelings?

Plan ahead and practice whenever possible. Share your feelings in small increments (i.e., piecemeal); don't dump them all at once. Emotional overload tends to short-circuit and overwhelm men.

Ask a man, "What is your reaction?" rather than, "What are you feeling?"

Think of communicating with a man as speaking your native language to someone from another culture. I have learned to do this with my foreign students, and they appreciate it.

Two wives shared with me how they helped their husbands with the communication process.

One said, "Honey, when I share my feelings with you, it's difficult for me to edit. I will probably talk too much and dump a load of emotions all over you. I just want you to know this in advance. You don't have to catch them all, just listen. If you want, I can repeat."

The other wife told her husband, "I appreciate you for sitting and listening to all this stuff. I'm not sure about all I just said. You probably feel the same way. Let's not talk now. Instead, let's think about it and then sort through everything later. What do you think?"

Both of these wives made it easier for their husbands. And the husbands appreciated their wife's responses.

CHAPTER 4

A Man *Is* His Work

My husband is having an affair!" She spit out the words as she sat in my office. Her angry look told me that her feelings had been building for some time.

"I just figured it out the other day," she continued. "He's been having this affair for the past several years. And it's not with a woman. It's with his job! That's his wife, his mistress! That's all he seems to live for. It's work, work, work! It gets the priorities; I get the leftovers. I get his worn-out carcass at night. Work gets his mind, his attention and his emotions, even when he's at home. I can tell by that preoccupied look on his face that he's still involved with his job, even when I'm talking with him."

She stopped for a minute and then went on, "And I'm not the only wife who feels this way. We've discussed this problem in our Bible study class and most of us are struggling with our husband's preoccupation with their work. Why can't husbands approach work like normal persons? Why do they get so involved? Why does it seem to consume their lives and have so much more meaning for them? Are there any answers? And more important, are there any solutions? I don't want the next 35 years of our life to be like this!"

Few men are free from the compulsion to work.

This woman has important questions—common questions that deserve an answer. Few men are free from the compulsion to work. The majority of men need to work. Often a man has a passionate and even painful love/hate affair with his job. Into his work he puts his competitive drives, his need to win, his aggression and his desperate search for his own identity.

Most men feel their work is more important than their wife's work. If a man believes his work defines who he is, then it's important that his wife's work be perceived as secondary to his. If your job requires that he give something up, don't be surprised if you meet him with some resistance. (There are many exceptions to this type of man, however.)

Too many men are defined by their work—and so is their status. The more important the job, the more it may pay; the higher the status, the greater the feeling of self-worth it confers. Outside recognition on the job can boost the man's estimation of himself. Employment is important. If the significant man in your life were unemployed, how would you feel? Think about it. If you're married and you were out with your husband and met someone, how would you feel if your husband's response to the question, "Well, what do you do?" was "Oh, I'm unemployed." Most wives are not against their husband's work. Rather, they are opposed to the lack of balance and meaning the work creates.

ENTRAPMENT OF WORK

Many men today are in a career trap. They may have trapped themselves into working so much because of economic desires. And then the pleasures of work become outweighed by the pain of overinvolvement.

They live with the phrase "work, work, work" screaming inside them, and they allow the words to become a command. Eventually they end up selling their lives, their wife, their children and their enjoyment for the position of a slave. Unfortunately, these are men who live with the motto "I am my job." This is a sad existence to live. Some of these men do wake up to their distorted value system, but it often takes a heart attack or the loss of family to do it. For a wife who is concerned about this tendency, creating a positive home life may bring about a change.

Please don't assume that all men like their jobs. The majority do not and wish they could do something else. Often they don't know what it would be, however. In Studs Terkel's classic book *Working*, only a handful of those interviewed liked their profession. This is sad and it creates stress for men and for those around them.

Women take more of a pragmatic approach to work. They see employment as a means to an end, but a man views employment as the end. Most everything in a man's world is connected to his work. If you were to ask a woman who she is, she would probably respond with a number of terms, describing her relationship with the world and the people around her. Not so a man. He would probably reply with a list of what he does and what he owns. This could include his house, car, clubs and associations, titles, duties, responsibilities and hobbies. A man's work is the way he can maintain all of these items.

INFATUATION OF WORK

Where did the infatuation with work begin? Probably when the man was a young boy. Most boys learn to value themselves in terms of achievements, successes and victories. Why? He most likely receives applause and rewards from his parents and friends as a boy when he runs faster, speaks better, reads earlier than others, wins a game, gets high grades or does anything that shows he's a "winner." From an early age men learn to respond to "You did a great job!" and "It'd be great if you did that well, too." When you're a winner, you're treated in a special way. Losing, failing or being incompetent brings rejection and disapproval. As the boy grows, he internalizes these parental attitudes and messages until they are his own inner voice that says nice things to him when he succeeds—or insults him when he doesn't.

If he doesn't achieve, he then draws on this reservoir of abuse, which can flood his lack of achievement. And what is unfortunate for many men, even when they do succeed, is that little voices break through and say, "But you could have done even better" or "So and so did a better job than you did."

All of this means that his emotions and moods are tied into his successes and failures. Elation comes from succeeding, and shame and embarrassment come from failing. You may not realize it since he has also learned to hide these feelings. He wants to protect his image and present a facade of one who is successful and in control.

PURPOSE OF WORK

Lifestyle and work—which one determines the other for men? Some men work to live and others live to work. There are a few men whose work fits their lifestyle, but for most, their lifestyle revolves around their job. My father worked hard to scrape together a living. He worked long hours and often six days a week. His daily routine when he arrived home was very predictable, as was his use of time on the weekends. Survival was very important to him as it was for anyone who came through the Great Depression.

Even though many men are married to their work, they are also married to a woman. And in today's world, a wife and children will not be content to exist with an absentee husband and father.

Today, work has taken on much more meaning for many men. It is what they do, where they do it and who they are. Ask a number of men what their work means to them, and you'll hear responses such as the following:

- "It's who I am."
- "It's my meal ticket."

- "It's a way to get to the top."
- "It's my way of not having to live like my parents did."
- "It's a calling from God."
- "It's my collegium. It's where I can butt heads with others and come out on top."
- "This is where my creativity shines. I can express myself through my job. I realize not everyone is that fortunate, but I am."

Ken Druck describes the potential of work very well when he says:

> Our work can be either a source of enormous personal fulfillment and liberation or a burial ground for some of our most disturbing fears and secrets. Work should be the stage on which many of our greatest performances in life are given and our most satisfying moments are lived. Men who love their work are often sustained by it through dry spells, loss of loved ones, sudden changes, or crises in other areas of their lives.[1]

There are numerous reasons why men work. A man works because God has called him to work. A person cannot really move through life adequately without working for just simple survival needs. Men work to express who they are. It's a way of saying to the world, "Here is what I do! This is what I have accomplished." A man steps back and looks at his achievement with a sense of satisfaction. He becomes less of a nameless face in the crowd through his accomplishments. It's a way to distinguish himself.

Men work to have a purpose for living. For some, work justifies living. Work provides meaning and significance. However, a balance is needed since so many men who retire at age 65 become depressed and even suicidal. Without work there is no meaning in life left for them.

Many men work to feel a part of something greater than themselves. Work provides them with relationships with others. A man feels good in providing for his family at home and also gets satisfaction through his teamwork contribution at work or

It doesn't matter whether you work with your mind or hands, body or thoughts, there is something satisfying about being able to express your abilities.

in society. Men and women have a need to contribute. God has called us to make a contribution to society and to others.

Work brings satisfaction. It doesn't matter whether you work with your mind or hands, body or thoughts, there is something satisfying about being able to express your abilities. Skills are refined by work, and even if a man is in a profession in which he doesn't always see the fruit of his labor, he can say, "I feel good just knowing that I worked today." I've heard men say, "Boy, I worked hard today, and I don't know what I accomplished. But it feels good just to be tired like this. It tells me I worked."

Work is an opportunity for men to make an impact and difference in their world. One man said to me, "When I die, I want my absence to be noticed for years to come. I want to change my community, my city and, yes, even the world in some way. You ask me why I work. That's why. I'm putting my brand on the world around me and it's going to stay. I want people to miss me."

A man works to improve his station in life. This can involve money to purchase those items that he feels he needs for the good life. His work brings recognition, a new status and respect.

Men work to enable themselves to move to a better neighborhood or to drive a sharper car that others will notice. They work so that their children will not have to go without, as they did. There is a drive to improve, which is good as long as it stays under their control and they don't allow it to control them.

These are just some of the reasons why men work, but before you read on, I would like you to do something. Take a piece of paper, and if you are married or have a close male friend, please do the following: Write down five reasons why you think your man works. Then say to him, "Have you ever identified the five major reasons why you work? I'd be interested in knowing what they are. I've written down five of my own reasons for why I think you work, and I'd like to see if I really know your motivation. When you write your reasons down, I'd like to hear them and then share my ideas with you." When he begins sharing, take it one step further. Ask him where he thinks those reasons were learned. Then ask him, "Ten years from now and then 20 years from now, why do you think you will be working? Will it be because of the same reasons or different ones?" I think you will have a very interesting conversation.

PITFALLS OF WORK

Men use work for other reasons, too. Have you ever considered how men use work as a hiding place? A man's work may not enrich his life as he hoped it would. Unfortunately, this can lead a man to use work to hide his feelings or not to live life to its fullest potential.

Work is a great place for a man to hide his feelings. The feelings that create a state of discomfort in a man can be buried and hidden by plunging into work.

Work can also become a hiding place for the fear of failure. How? Some men ward off their concern over failing by staying busy. If a man senses failure or feels that he isn't doing as much as others, he can accelerate his time at work. It's a great way to hide his inner sense of inadequacy. This type of behavior, however, sets a precedent that others may come to expect, and the man soon finds himself on a treadmill to nowhere.

Work is often used as an excuse not to live life more fully in other ways. What better way to avoid intimacy than by working unusually long hours? After all, when a man works that much, how can you expect him to have time, energy and interest in people, relationships and family events?

Work also becomes the hiding place for the man who feels inadequate. Work enables him to be a man. This equation leads a man to use his work as a proving ground. And the more insecure a man is about himself, the harder he works. Compulsive work patterns are often the result of inner-driving insecurities.

Have you ever heard a man say, "Of course I love my family and they ought to know it. Just look how hard I work for them!"? Bringing home the paycheck is the only expression of love that some men know. The love expressed through responsibility is usually indicative of a man who does not know how to express his love in other ways. For such men, showing love is easier than expressing it verbally.[2]

CONCERNS ABOUT WORK AND FAMILY

Listen to what some men have said concerning work and family-related responsibilities:

> I would like my wife to show appreciation in recognizing the pressures we men go through and the responsibilities of being the provider and caretaker—not only financially, but in the spiritual, emotional, social and mental areas as well. As a man, my concentration is on the overall picture and goals. It's true that some of the attention to detail gets lost in the shuffle. But what I do is often misunderstood, and the appreciation for what I am doing gets lost.

> I want to feel needed and know I am important at home. I'm sensitive to not only what is said but also how it is said. Criticism shuts me down. It would help if our wives who are full-time homemakers and haven't worked in the competitive, chaotic work world outside of the home could understand that it is difficult and challenging for Christian men to interact and work under the constant influences of non-Christian attitudes all day.

> Do women really understand how we feel about the responsibility for making ends meet? Their actions tell us they don't. We feel burdened to provide for the family, whether our wives are employed or not. Many of us

fear disappointing the family and failing in our roles of protector, provider, father, family leader and spiritual head. Our self-worth, our egos and our identities are linked to both work and home. It often appears that we are not as interested in what goes on at home as we are with what happens at work. That may not always be the case—we may just be exhausted from work. It is frustrating for us not to have more time to give of ourselves at home.

Right or wrong, good or bad, like it or not, a man does use his work to build his identity.

It's true. Right or wrong, good or bad, like it or not, a man does use his work to build his identity. He uses his work to express who he is just as a woman finds other ways to express who she is. And yes, work also gives a man a purpose for his life, and for many it's satisfying. In William Hendricks and Doug Sherman's book *Your Work Matters to God*, they discuss biblical purposes for working:

> Through work we serve people, through work we meet our own needs, through work we meet our families' needs, through work we earn money to give to others, through work we love God.[3]

These are the reasons the man in your life works! Listen carefully when he shares his concerns about his work.

SUGGESTIONS FOR A MORE BALANCED LIFE

The following eight scenarios and suggestions are provided to inspire you and your man to try new ways of handling your man's balance between work and family responsibilities.

Scenario 1

"Sometimes I feel like my wife has no idea how stressful my job can be," said one man. "When I come home, I am tired and just want to relax. I wish that she would try to support me more at what I do rather than always expecting me to help her with chores around the house as soon as I come in the door. If she showed more interest in supporting me at my job, I would be more interested in helping her around the house."

Suggestion 1

Encourage your husband to make a list of the various work pressures he faces, or you make a list of potential work pressures and ask him to check off the main ones that apply to his job situation. Then ask how you can help. One wife asked to go to work with her husband for a day and just observe what he had to deal with. She told him beforehand she wouldn't make suggestions or comments unless he asked her to do so. It may help sometime to turn on a tape recorder at home to record an interchange. This has helped many discover whether what they say is constructive and supportive or critical and unsupportive.

Scenario 2

One man said, "I long to be appreciated for who I am, especially at home. I want to experience unconditional love at home—not just performance-based love. I struggle with that all day long on the job. When I come home, I don't always want to hear how hard my wife has worked. I need to hear some loving compliments, not just complaints! If I hear something uplifting first, I can problem solve better."

Suggestion 2

One wife made a point of either telling or writing a note stating how much she appreciates what the man in her life accomplishes. A grateful daughter took the time to write her father a letter expressing appreciation for all he had done for her. If you're a wife, you may want to practice the "four-minute drill" at the end of the day when you first see your husband. During the initial four minutes, make it a point to touch, hug, affirm, be friendly and be positive. Save the complaints about "his kids" and the broken plumbing until after he's eaten dinner. Remember, what takes place during the first four minutes when you see each other at the end of the workday sets the tone for the rest of the evening. If it's positive, it tends to continue in that direction. If it's negative—need I say more?

Scenario 3

One man said, "I would love for my wife to give me a hug and a kiss (without having to ask for one or be the initiator) and to ask me to share what's going on in my head. And after I'm done unloading all my concerns and worries, not to offer advice, unless asked, but instead pray with me for God's guidance. This would help me release all my anxieties to God and provide a clean heart for my family."

Another man said, "It would be nice if she and I could sit down at the end of the day and review the highlights—to share what I really think without having her making judgments about the people I work with. It would be nice to have a sounding board—someone to just bounce ideas off of who doesn't judge. I would value her honest opinion."

Suggestion 3

These men are looking for their wives to be a support. In a case like this, ask your man how he wants you to pray for him in the morning before he goes to work, and then send him an e-mail or leave a message on his voice mail that you're praying for him. Too often phone or other messages to a man at work are "I need your advice" or "Something needs fixing."

Scenario 4

A 40-year-old man said, "I think I am still a big kid at heart. I would like my wife to give me more encouragement regarding my business life and my home life. Maybe more 'that-a-boys,' 'thank yous' or 'good jobs.' I am at a level in my company where I don't get it at the office. I do get some appreciation at home, but that kid in me needs more."

Suggestion 4

Have you ever asked who your man's encouragers are at work? Or how he would like to be encouraged by others at work? If your husband is an extrovert, he's the type of person who may think he's done a good job but won't really believe it until he's heard it from someone else. Therefore, even if you've already said it once this week, you may need to say it again. It may help to find out if he prefers to hear it privately or in front of others.

Scenario 5

As one man put it, "I need continual affirmation that I am a good father and husband. I never had any training in being either one. I guess I need the acknowledgment that I am doing the best I can, even if I don't quite measure up to all my wife's desires and expectations. Please don't compare me to other fathers! I'm not them. We're all different and need some help. Give me physical affection and let me know you're glad you married me. Sometimes I worry about this."

Suggestion 5

It's easy to look around and compare what you don't have. It's very deflating to a man to be compared, even in a joking way. Men have to live with comparisons and competition all of their lives. They don't want this from their wives too. It's a personal affront to them. Instead, you can encourage your man if he feels lacking in some areas by saying, "You know, we all do the best we can with the limited knowledge that we have. I do appreciate that. Are you comfortable with what you know now or would you like to become even more proficient?"

Scenario 6

"The thing I want her to do the minute I walk in the door," said one man, "is not to hit me with instantaneous decisions. But how would I feel if I had been with small children all day? I also would like her to give me some more around-the-house responsibilities so that she has more time for me. She often is still folding clothes through the 10 o'clock news, after which we retire. Often I seem to be the last on her list."

Suggestion 6

It's true! Many men feel they get the leftovers after their children.

There are solutions, though. Suggest these solutions and give him a choice. Let your man know you want time alone with him. This can happen if:

1. You hire a babysitter for one hour each evening.
2. You work out a plan together to simplify some of the tasks.
3. He could help with some of the tasks, which would give you some free time.

Scenario 7

"I'm like many men," one man admits, "I love to create and build. Yes, I'm the one who watches *Home Improvement*. I like to work on the house, the barbecue grill, the boat and the lawn. I enjoy serving my wife in this way, but it sure would help if she explained what she wanted before I completed the project. It's disheartening and demotivating to have to make changes once the job is finished."

Suggestion 7

Be sure you've clarified and decided exactly what you want done before your man gets involved. Once a man gets started on a project, he's single-minded. It throws him when changes occur, and if he hears after the fact that you would have preferred something else, he will interpret it as a personal criticism that he blew it. He will feel like his efforts were not appreciated.

Scenario 8

One man said, "Before my wife can demonstrate understanding, encouragement or acceptance of my struggles, she needs to *make time* to talk in order to discover what they are. I know that this is a priority that we must share together. However, I do feel like a lower priority in my wife's life (after the needs of the children, her church commitments and time spent with her friends) than she is in mine. I guess if I had to request only one thing, I would like my wife to change her tone of voice when she speaks to me. Her predominant tone is critical, negative and belittling."

Another man said, "I guess an encouragement for me would be if my wife worked at taking the 'log out of her own eye' so she could help me with mine. Then I could really trust her statements of understanding. I feel like I am working to get healthier, and as head of the family, it should probably start with me—I'm glad it does anyway. I feel she has yet to really start, so it's harder for her to comprehend and understand. When I know myself better and when she's begun to understand me, then I will feel like her statements and support will mean more, and I will be able to trust and receive them with more confidence. Too often now I feel that what I share comes back to 'hit' me at a later date. I'm working to process that and deal with this issue with her. Not having to worry about when I'll get hit again would be a relief and encouragement."

Suggestion 8

This is a common issue between husbands and wives. To reiterate an earlier point, I am not trying to let men off the hook. They share in these problems quite often by not being available, not sharing or by being defensive. However, at times, you may need to be the one to take the initiative and start a new, more healthier way of communicating.

The bottom line is this: You can't wait for the other person to change before you respond in new ways.

CHAPTER 5

What Men Want from Women

(Besides Sex)

Responses and Suggestions

The purpose of this chapter is to discover how a woman can impact her man through deliberate acts of nurturing, defending, taking initiative, encouraging and understanding.

CREATE A SAFE ENVIRONMENT

Response

The one thing that I would like my wife to do is to encourage me—to create for me a place in her arms or in my home that is a shelter from the things I'm dealing with, not a place with more demands or expectations, or a place where she personally suggests how I should deal with things (unless I solicit her opinion). Her encouragement would be in the form of words and actions. Her words would say "You're doing so well." "You can do it." "I know what you do will be the best." Her actions would include finding ways to lighten my load or just saying okay and doing something I suggest. Agreeing with me would be another form of encouragement. Encouraging me to be myself would indicate to me that she accepts me, rather than always trying to change me. Wanting me different means not accepting who I am.

Suggestion 1: Don't Offer Unsolicited Advice

A wife often tries to improve her husband's responses or help him by offering unsolicited advice. As strange as it seems, when a woman offers unsolicited advice to a man, he tends not to see it as helpful but rather interprets it as *You don't know what to do; you need my help.* If the man came from a home in which he was criticized as a child, he will activate those leftover responses to his present relationship. Even if they're not, men like to think of themselves as experts. It is man's desire to be proficient and in control. And if you suggest that he listen to the advice of an expert, he could really be upset.[1]

His response to you may be that he feels unloved because he feels you're not trusting him. You could say, "I've got a suggestion if you're interested. You let me know if you are."

When a woman offers unsolicited advice to a man, he tends not to see it as helpful.

Suggestion 2: Encourage, Don't Discourage

A wife also may try to change or control her husband's behavior by talking about how upset she is or letting him know her negative feelings. Again, his thought is, *She doesn't love me, because she doesn't accept me the way I am.* Your requested change may be quite insightful, but it's not packaged in a way that is heard. Sharing the request in a positive way, pointing to the desired response or even expressing it in writing often works better.

Do you find yourself noticing or acknowledging what your husband has done? Or instead do you comment on what has *not* been accomplished? That's discouraging and disheartening. Naturally, he feels unappreciated and taken for granted. Men and women want their *efforts* to be recognized and valued. Appreciation is the best way to see the desired behavior continue.

Men want to feel successful. They want to be successful in their male-female relationships. Yet too often they end up feeling like a failure, which is very discouraging. It's easy to give up and withdraw.

Consider what four men said about this issue:

Many of us would like to communicate with our wives as intimately as they communicate with their friends. But we find it difficult. Who will help us learn? We receive few offers—only complaints.

Women say we are single-minded. We are. Single-mindedness helps us reach our goals. We have difficulty listening when we are concentrating on something else. We are accused of being purposely inattentive and made to feel guilty and even attacked for this. Why?

We want women to understand that we need more time to process what is said to us than women do. When we feel pressured to be different, we may use anger as our protection—to get others to back off.

She expects me to have these reactions right at my fingertips and be able to call them up on the spot. Well, I can't do that. I don't operate the way she does. I need a little more time to think things through. I don't want to say something I'm going to regret later on. Somehow she has the idea that wanting time to think is not being open and honest with her. That is ridiculous! I'm not trying to hide anything. I'm just trying to be sure in my own mind before I talk to her about it.

Here are some statements you can use, not only to help a man communicate and to encourage him, but also to instruct him in a nonthreatening way:

- "I really feel safe when I share my feelings with you."
- "It really helps me solve problems and fix things when you listen to me."
- "I appreciate how you help me arrive at my own solutions to some of my problems!"
- "I really feel affirmed by you when you see my opinion as having validity. Sometimes I really need your perspective."
- "I like it when you let me problem solve out loud and find the solution. I know you have some good ideas; holding them back must be hard at times."
- "I want to take three minutes and tell you what happened. I think you'll find these details interesting and pertinent to this incident."

One of the statements *not* to make is, "You don't understand." This not only discourages a man but frustrates him. He then tends to tune out whatever your explanation is going to be. If he doesn't catch what you've said, you could say, "Let me put it another way." Then be sure to put it in his language and keep it brief.[2]

DEFEND YOUR MAN

Response

Defend me—not in a way that says I'm always right, but in a way that indicates she knows I'm really trying. There is a lot of criticism of men in today's society. I want to know my wife is on my side, not on the side that is critical. And I must say, I believe she is. For that I am grateful.

Suggestion

Making the statement, "I believe in you," or putting a note in your husband's pocket can be helpful. Watch the questions you ask, because a man may think you're judging him. Preface your questions with, "I want to understand what you're experiencing. That's why I'm asking these questions."

TAKE THE INITIATIVE

Response

There is also a strong connection between a man's sex drive and his ego. Women need to know how they impact us. The way they dress, wiggle, look or touch us affects us. We struggle continuously with keeping our sex lives pure, especially when our wives are cold. Sometimes we don't want to be romantic; we just want to have sex. Other times we need to know we are desired, loved and accepted. We enjoy having our wives take the initiative.

Suggestion

Be as attractive as possible, and initiate and discuss what, how and when your man likes to make love.

ENCOURAGE YOUR MAN

Responses

Three men in a small group were asked what their wives could do to encourage them. They were quite specific in what they said:

I would just love for my wife to ask questions that would lead to a greater understanding of who I am and what I have to deal with daily. I believe this would lead to a greater appreciation of me.

Just to have her assure me that she will support and love me no matter what happens—even if I lose my job or I am uncertain about what to do next with my life—and to affirm that God is in control and she is trusting Him to care for both of us.

Women like to vent their feelings to a listening spouse without editorials or comments. I would like my wife to draw out my feelings about a situation but never editorialize or attempt to define what I mean. Next Tuesday evening after thinking about a specific situation, I may change my mind 180 degrees. I would like to be allowed to mull over things without being thought of as rude or disinterested.[3]

I asked this specific question to a group of men: What could your wife do to encourage and support you more? Here are a few of the responses I received:

It would be nice if she would initiate lovemaking from time to time. However, the mitigating circumstances are our three sons, ages five, four and two. She has little energy left over most days.

I would love for her to be more consistent in assisting me with everyday details that make up our days, such as dinner, laundry, housecleaning and paying bills. Through these helps, she encourages me that I'm not alone.

It would encourage me if she would comment on the things that I do as favors, because I am wanting to help out. She tends to see my efforts to help as obligations that I should be doing anyway.

I would like my wife to encourage me when I am down, distraught, overwhelmed and beaten. I don't need her advice nor any sympathy. I just need to hear her gently say to me, "Honey, I know you are hurting. I may not be able to help you solve your problem, but tell me what is bothering you. Let's ask the Father to help you and comfort you." And most of all, it would encourage me if she gave me time to "brew over it."

I want her to be more encouraging and truly desirous of giving encouragement rather than focusing on her own difficulties. And to be more encouraging in the sense that she's on my side rather than an adversary, or putting me on the defensive by saying, "Why didn't you say . . . ?" or "Why did you do that?"

By avoiding reminding me that something should be obvious to me and asking why I brought it up. By being more mindful of my need for touching or hugging, even if it's not obvious that I need it. By being more receptive and grateful for even the small things that I do to let her know I am thinking of her.

Suggestion
In a national survey, which included more than 300 men of all ages, this is what they said in response to the statement "I would appreciate it if my partner would . . . ." You may be surprised

at some of the items that received responses of "important" or "very important."

Ninety to 100 percent of the men said listening to their ideas and being fun to be around were at the top of their list. Eighty to 90 percent wanted their wives to listen to their concerns, verbally saying, "I love you," show appreciation for what their husbands do for them, show independence and pursue their own interests.[4]

Reread the men's responses. You will find many new ways to encourage your man in ways that men prefer.

UNDERSTAND YOUR MAN'S FEELINGS

There is one last subject that is a source of tension, controversy and difference between men and women. Men have strong concerns about this issue—their feelings.

Responses

We're always taking hits about emotions, feelings or whatever you call them. There is confusion here for both men and women. We are emotional beings. We are not as insensitive as we are stereotyped to be, but we have difficulty moving from the logical/linear side of the mind to the emotional side if we are left-brained males. Not all of us are left-brained either.[5] (See ch. 1.)

Stereotypes limit us. Women are convinced that all men think about is power and sex, or sex and power! So when we do open up emotionally, our response is automatically classified to one of these areas.[6] (See ch. 1.)

I would say many women don't understand the reality and depth of emotional pain men feel, especially when it relates to feelings of inadequacy imposed by society's markings of a real man—financial success, sexual potency, physical stature, competency and so on. I wonder if the average wife knows how much her husband needs her support, admiration and affirmation.[7] (See ch. 1.)

My wife says things to me that hurt deeply. She says them in passing without much emotion or anger, just off the cuff. She seems to say them at times when discussion would be inappropriate (e.g., when other people are present). Finally, when we do get time to talk, the hurt is less severe or I just let it pass. This is probably more my problem than hers.[8] (See ch. 1.)

We struggle with emotions and stress. It seems that women, even those from the feminist groups, feel that they have all the stress. I don't know if they understand the gigantic responsibility we face being God's umbrella of protection for our families in a world that has such great negative influence and unhealthy attractions. It is hard to keep all your ducks in a straight line at times.[9] (See ch. 1.)

Suggestion 1: Consider the Differences
Let's consider this issue right away: feelings and emotions. Recently I came across Michael Gurian's fascinating book *The Wonder of Boys*. I wish every parent could grasp the information in this book. One section was entitled, "How Boys Experience Their Feelings and Emotions." (Keep in mind that the reason for male and female differences goes back to the presence of testosterone in men, as well as the difference in their brain structures.)

Boys have seven internal processing methods for experiencing feelings and emotions. You may see a number of these methods in the men in your life:

1. They have an *active-release approach*. They process and express their feelings through some sort of action like a game or activity, or even yelling. Have you ever seen this occur?

2. Then there's the *suppression-delayed reaction method*. A male is wired differently. Whereas a woman may verbally process a problem aloud immediately, men are basically wired for a more delayed reaction. A man's brain is a problem-solving brain, so emotional reactions are delayed until the problem is solved. He may be irritable at this time, but he doesn't talk about the problem. Perhaps you've experienced this in your relationship with your husband, father or son.

3. Men also engage in the *displacement-objectification method*. Perhaps a boy or a man is angry. You want him to talk about it, but he won't. He might first talk about how someone else feels in a particular dilemma. Once he does that, he may then talk about how he feels.

   Boys tend to relate objects even to their feelings since that's safer. One boy saw a dog chained up. He said, "Boy, what a life. He's tied down and stuck there. Can't go where he wants to and feels like everybody is pulling his chain. Sometimes that's the way I feel when . . . "

   Once again, he needs more time to deal with the feelings. That's how you can encour-

age him. He may need you to help him connect his feelings to the outside world. A wife
realized that her husband had a difficult day
at work because he was unusually quiet.
Since his responses were unusually short, she
discovered he had an overload of problems at
work. She said, "It sounds like you had an
experience today like the red sports car I read
about at the wild animal park."

He said, "What are you talking about?"

"Well, it's that drive-through park where
the animals roam around. A guy drove
through the park in his red sports car and one
of the elephants who worked in a circus saw
it. The elephant came over and sat down on it
like he had been taught to do in the circus."

Her husband replied, "You couldn't
have put it any more aptly. I felt just like
that car, except my elephant jumped up and
down a bit!"

4. Yet another method of dealing with feelings is the
physical expression method, which boys use much more
than girls. Exercise and games provide some of the
outlets for their inner feelings. Again, you can see
how men use action rather than words. You've probably heard the expression "Going in the cave."
Several writers, including John Gray, the author of
Men Are from Mars, Women Are from Venus, address this
issue. On average, boys don't process their feelings as
quickly as girls. Sometimes it takes them several
hours to do so. (You may be thinking, *It's more like
days!*) And they can become overwhelmed by a

woman's feelings. They prefer isolation so that they can sort out their feelings. They need to know it's okay to go into their cave, and it's okay to come out of their cave as well. Do you know a cave dweller? If so, do you try to drag him out of his cave, or do you encourage him to enter it and stay there awhile?

5. Another method men like to use is called *talking about feelings*. It's often easier for a boy or a man to talk about his feelings after an event rather than during it. You need to remember that it is physically more difficult for men to express feelings because of their brain structure. This isn't an excuse. It's the way God created males and females. It was His idea. You can encourage a man to talk about his feelings, but what may come naturally for you may feel awkward for him

6. The *problem solving method* is a process that often releases a boy's emotional energy. This is why you can expect the man in your life to move in this direction as quickly as possible. You may talk it out, but he wants to solve it. Seeing a problem creates feelings. When the problem is solved, he feels much better.

7. The *crying method* feels unsafe to boys or men. Culture has helped to keep men's tears pent up. Men do cry, but many of them can only cry on the inside. Only a few feel comfortable enough to express tears. The feeling of loss of control when this happens is an unpleasant exposure and vulnerability for most men.[10]

Suggestion 2: Validate His Feelings

Men are very skilled at covering up their real feelings. They have numerous ways of hiding their emotions. For example, when a man is sad, fearful, hurt or feeling guilty, he may use anger to avoid the pain of those feelings. When he's angry, he feels more like he's in control. And since most people don't feel like getting close to someone who is angry, he is able to maintain a safe distance.

When a man is sad, fearful, hurt or feeling guilty, he may use anger to avoid the pain of those feelings.

Then when a man is truly angry, in order to get away from the pain of those feelings, he may use discouragement or indifference as his Novocain.

When a man is insecure, uncertain, feeling ashamed or actually afraid, anger is useful to avoid facing those feelings. He may turn his anger into aggression to overcompensate for other feelings he can't safely express.

One of the most frequent translations of one feeling for another is the exchange of anger for frustration. Thus, one of the best responses you can give a man about what he is experiencing or feeling is validation. Do you understand what "validation" means? It's the process or act of confirming or supporting the meaningfulness and relevance of what your man is feeling. It's listening and understanding his perspective. It's walking with him emotionally without trying to change the direction he is going.[11]

Suggestion 3: Don't Edit Your Own Feelings
One of the mistakes some women make is to edit *their own* feelings,

because they believe their men can't handle them. They try to protect their husbands, fathers or sons from their pain when they're upset. If you hold back your feelings because your man has difficulty handling them, you're not helping the relationship; you're creating an emotional distance. It will leave you starving for emotional connection—from anyone! This is one of the reasons why some women stray from their husbands.

When you edit or block your feelings, you begin to lose your own identity. You may end up being unsure of whether you are the person who experienced that emotion or whether you're another person who is trying not to feel it. It's like asking yourself, *Who am I? Who's the real me? Am I the one who feels or the one who doesn't feel?*

The result is, some women don't encourage their men with positive affirmations because of the confusion they have over their own feelings.[12]

Suggestion 4: Be Patient and Trustworthy

Remember that when a man does share his feelings with you, it's often difficult for him. It's also a big step, because most men have not learned a feeling vocabulary, nor are they adept at giving word pictures. It would be helpful to him if you recognized his attempts and progress. When he shares his feelings with you, refrain from judging or criticizing him. Remember that the way he shares as well as the amount he shares probably won't be the same way or amount you share. That's all right. You're not to be his instructor at this time.

In addition, he may stop to think about what he wants to say. Don't fill in the silent times. In your heart and mind give him all the time he needs to formulate what is happening inside him.

Since it is a step in vulnerability to share his feelings with you, keep what is said in confidence. Let him know you will do this. He doesn't want your mother, his mother or your friends to know.

When feelings are shared, he may simply state them and not offer them up for discussion. Either let him lead in this or ask him if he wants you to listen or respond.

When you want to know what he is feeling, ask, "What's your reaction to this?" rather than, "What are you feeling?" He can respond best to the first question.

Suggestion 5: Don't Interrupt

Never—I mean, never—interrupt. I remember the first occasion I shared with my wife, Joyce, about the times when I had been depressed. I sat at the dining-area table and Joyce stood 30 feet away with her back to me, washing the dishes. When I started sharing, she stopped what she was doing, came over, sat down and listened. Never once did she interrupt or make a value judgment on what I was sharing. I felt safe.

Interruptions cause men to retreat and think, *Why bother sharing?*

Interruptions cause men to retreat and think, *Why bother sharing?* Always remember, sharing feelings takes more effort, energy and concentration for men than it does for women. Men need to stay focused on one thing at a time. Interruptions throw them off course, and because they are goal conscious, they like to stay on course and complete the process.

Distractions make it difficult for a man to sort through the time-consuming process of interpreting his emotions. Many men are not emotionally articulate, because they lack language skills in this area. When you are patient and accept this lack of skills, it helps your man talk more.

A wife shared with me a commitment note she gave her husband. She said it brought about the emotional interchange she had wanted for years. The note read:

> Since sharing your emotions with me is such a cherished experience and so vital to a wonderful sexual relationship, I commit myself to you to respond in the following manner: When you share, you can count on me to listen, not expect you to describe your feelings exactly as I do, not interrupt, not make value judgments. And finally, if we do enter into a discussion, I will limit my participation to 15 minutes.

To say the least, her husband was very encouraged.

Two days later she received a dozen roses and a note that said, "Thank you. My commitment when you share is 'ditto.' I won't try to solve the problem unless you ask me to."

Suggestion 6: Practice Scriptural Values

There are wonderful scriptural guidelines for the way you interact with the man in your life. There is a right time to speak and a time to be quiet. Proverbs 10:19 emphasizes this:

> In a multitude of words transgression is not lacking, but he who restrains his lips is prudent (*AMP*).

The Living Bible is graphic in its rendering of this verse:

Don't talk so much. You keep putting your foot in your mouth. Be sensible and turn off the flow!

Proverbs 17 speaks of a man as knowledgable who holds his tongue:

> He who has knowledge spares his words, and a man of understanding has a cool spirit. Even a fool when he holds his peace is considered wise; when he closes his lips he is esteemed a man of understanding (vv. 27-28, *AMP*).

Being hasty means blurting out what you are thinking without considering the effect it will have on others:

> Do you see a man who is hasty in his words? There is more hope for a [self-confident] fool than for him (Prov. 29:20, *AMP*).

The word "edify," which is part of helping, means to hold up or to promote growth in Christian wisdom, grace, virtue and holiness. Romans 14:19 emphasizes this:

> So let us then definitely aim for and eagerly pursue what makes for harmony and for mutual upbuilding (edification and development) of one another (*AMP*).

Suggestion 7: Speak Positively

A wife may correct what her husband says or does and tell him what to do and how to do something. However, he probably won't respond well to her directions, especially if he does not feel admired. When a wife challenges, criticizes or corrects her husband's decisions or initiations (especially in front of others), he feels unloved, angry and humiliated. He wants to be encouraged to do things on his own. Instead, ask if he would like to hear an observation, and if he doesn't, let it go. When a wife shares her displeasure by asking questions that carry an accusatory tone, implying, "You blew it," she can count on a defensive response.

Common defense-producing questions include How could you? and Why in the world did you do that? A man will feel unaccepted, unapproved and unloved, and definitely not encouraged when questions are asked or statements made, such as the following:

- "How can you think of buying that? You already have two and you rarely use them."
- "Those dishes are still wet. They'll be dry streaked unless you redo them."
- "Your hair is getting kind of ragged, isn't it?"
- "There's a parking spot over there. Turn around quickly and go over there."
- "You shouldn't work so hard. None of the other men does."
- "Don't put that there. It will get lost."
- "You should call an electrician. He'll know what to do."
- "Why are we waiting for a table? Didn't you call ahead?"
- "You should spend more time with your sons. They miss you."
- "Your office is still a mess. How can you think in here? When are you going to clean it up?"
- "You forgot to bring it home again. Maybe you could write yourself a note."
- "You're driving too fast. Slow down."

- "Next time we should read the movie reviews; this wasn't good."
- "I didn't know what time to expect you. You should have called."
- "Somebody drank from the milk bottle again. Don't eat with your fingers. You're setting a bad example for the kids."

These statements will elicit a response, but probably not the one you want.

You will notice a less defensive and more positive response from your man if you share your concern in a calm voice, saying, "I am upset, and I don't want to be. Help me to understand what is happening. I need your perspective." Your man will more easily accept this positive speech rather than accusing or critical speech.

For additional responses from men regarding how they'd like their wives to understand them better and accept them, see chapter 7.

CHAPTER 6

What Can You Do? Pray

People today are into power. Perhaps it's always been that way. Most of us though have never really availed ourselves of a means of power that can change our lives—our own lives and others' lives. There is a tremendous power in prayer.

How are you praying for the men in your life? How do you pray for your husband, boyfriend, father or son? Would you call yourself a woman of prayer?

God's Word has so much to say to us about prayer. God wants us to talk with Him. He is just waiting to respond.

It shall come to pass that before they call, I will answer; and while they are still speaking, I will hear (Isa. 65:24, *NKJV*).

Then you will call upon Me and go and pray to Me, and I will listen to you (Jer. 29:12, *NKJV*).

Call to Me, and I will answer you, and show you great and mighty things, which you do not know (Jer. 33:3, *NKJV*).

WHAT IS PRAYER?

In order for prayer to truly impact our lives, we need to understand what prayer is. Stormie Omartian gives us a helpful description:

Prayer is much more than just giving a list of desires to God, as if He were the great Sugar Daddy/Santa Claus in the sky. Prayer is acknowledging and experiencing the presence of God and inviting His presence into our lives and circumstances. It's seeking the presence of God and releasing the power of God which gives us the means to overcome any problem.

The Bible says, "Whatever you bind on earth will be bound in heaven, and whatever you loose on earth will be loosed in heaven" (Matthew 18:18). God gives us authority on earth. When we take that authority, God releases power to us from heaven. Because it's God's power and not ours, we become the vessel through which His power flows. When we pray, we bring that power to bear upon everything we are praying about, and we allow the power of God to work through our powerlessness. When we pray, we are humbling ourselves before God and saying, "I need Your presence and Your power, Lord, I can't do this without You." When we don't pray, it's like saying we have no need of anything outside ourselves.

Praying in the name of Jesus is a major key to God's power. Jesus said, "Most assuredly, I say to you, whatever you ask the Father in My name He will give to you" (John 16:23). Praying in the name of Jesus gives us authority over the enemy and proves we have faith in God to do what His Word promises. God knows our thoughts and our needs, but He responds to our prayers. That's because He always gives us a choice about everything, including whether we will trust Him by praying in Jesus' name.

Prayer can not only encourage the one you are praying for, but it can also encourage and change you.

Praying not only affects us, it also reaches out and touches those for whom we pray. When we pray for others, we are asking God to make His presence a part of their lives and work powerfully in their behalf. That doesn't mean there will always be an immediate response. Sometimes it can take days, weeks, months or even years. But our prayers are never lost or meaningless. If we are praying, something is happening whether we can see it or not. The Bible says, "The effective, fervent prayer of a righteous man avails much" (James 5:16). All that needs to happen in our lives cannot happen without the presence and power of God. Prayer invites and ignites both.[1]

Praying for a man is *not* a means of gaining control over him. Prayer is a means of transforming people—both the one who is praying and the one who is the object of the prayers. Not only can prayer encourage the one you are praying for, but it can also encourage and change you.

HOW DOES PRAYER OVERCOME?

There may be times when it's difficult to pray for a man—it could be your husband. You may *not* want to pray for him. You could be angry or even bitter toward him, and the last thing you want to do is encourage him or pray for him. However, an amazing thing happens when you bring another person before the Lord. Your attitude begins to change. Bitterness decreases, anger diminishes and hardness toward the other softens. In time you can end up loving the person you are praying for. I've seen relationships restored between daughters and fathers, wives and husbands, and mothers and sons. It may take time, but prayer is the means of restoration, growth and encouragement.

Stormie Omartian, in her book *The Power of a Praying Wife*, shares a struggle with her husband's anger that she experienced:

I began to pray every day for Michael, like I had never prayed before. Each time, though, I had to confess my own hardness of heart. I saw how deeply hurt and unforgiving of him I was. *I don't want to pray for him. I don't want to ask God to bless him. I only want God to strike his heart with lightning and convict him of how cruel he has been,* I thought. I had to say over and over, "God, I confess my unforgiveness toward my husband. Deliver me from all of it."

Little by little, I began to see changes occur in both of us. When Michael became angry, instead of reacting negatively, I prayed for him. I asked God to give me insight into what was causing his rage. He did. I asked Him what I could do to make things better. He showed me. My husband's anger became less frequent and more quickly soothed. Every day, prayer built something positive. We're still not perfected, but we've come a long way. It hasn't been easy, yet I'm convinced that God's way is worth the effort to walk in it.[2]

One of the ways that my wife, Joyce, has helped me over the years is through prayer. When I am traveling and speaking, I know that when I call home each evening I will hear her say, "I'll be praying for you as you're teaching tomorrow." I'll also find notes stuck in my pockets (and elsewhere) saying, "I'm praying for you," as well as a Scripture verse written out.

Over the years I've made it a practice to pray for my clients each day. I usually let them know that I will be doing this and ask if they have something specific they would like me to pray about during the week. I've had a number of occasions when a person has later shared that the only thing that kept them going was knowing that at least one person was praying for them.

HOW CAN YOU PRAY SPECIFICALLY FOR YOUR MAN?

If you're married, what are some ways you can pray for your husband?

Carole Mayhall, writing in *Today's Christian Woman*, suggests the following:

How to Pray "Just for Him"

Make it a point to commit five minutes a day to pray just for your husband. Pray a different Scripture for him each month, as well as other specific requests that God puts on your heart. And keep a prayer list specifically for him. The list might look something like this:

For my husband: (put the date you begin praying)

Colossians 1:9-11

- That he would be filled with the knowledge of God's will.
- That he would have spiritual wisdom and understanding.
- That he would have a life worthy of God.
- That he would be strengthened with God's power for patience and endurance.
- That he would have a thankful spirit.
- That he would develop a friendship with a committed Christian who would challenge him.
- That God would give him a hunger and thirst for himself and his Word.

Write down the answers when they come and date them.

After a friend of mine had been praying specifically for her husband for several months, she called me, excitement lilting in her voice. "Guess what!" she exclaimed. "Bill just told me a new co-worker asked him if he'd be willing to attend a new early morning Bible study, and Bill said YES! And something else. I tried not to show my astonishment when Bill brought home a brochure on a Marriage Enrichment weekend and said he'd signed us up to go."

My friend and I rejoiced together in this new beginning.[3]

Another woman shared her story of how God answered prayer for her friend's husband:

While visiting my friend Barbara in Germany last spring, I listened fascinated one evening as her husband Russell, an Air Force officer, explained to a group packed into their dining room about the meaning of the Passover meal we were about to eat. As a Bible study teacher, he had spent hours preparing the lesson, the food and the table.

After we'd eaten, I helped Barbara in the kitchen. "Russ is really turned onto the Lord!" I exclaimed. "I still remember the Sunday years ago when you asked me to pray for him. He was so wrapped up in his career he had no time for God, and he was so reserved—almost stiff in those days. But now, he is not only a mighty man of God, he's a terrific Bible teacher. What did you do besides pray a lot during the time he wasn't following the Lord?"

As Barbara shared, I jotted down her answers:

1. I had many intercessors join me in praying for him.
2. I was single-minded in my goal—determined that my words and my behavior would make him thirsty for the Lord. I asked the Lord to keep His joy bubbling out of me.
3. Russ liked to show off our home and my cooking by having company over, so I often invited Christians to share meals with us. He enjoyed that—especially meeting Christian men, whom he found fun to be around.
4. The children and I kept going to church.
5. Russ began to go with me to a Bible study—probably out of curiosity, but also because I had such joy. Then he started going to church with the family.

Russ finally decided to make Jesus his personal Lord. He immediately had a hunger to know the Word of God and began spending hours each week studying the Bible. Now he's teaching a Bible study group that meets in their home.

I observed Russell's tender heart toward God during my visit with them, and thanked the Lord for doing such a "good job" in answering a wife's prayers for her husband.[4]

HOW CAN YOU PERSONALIZE SCRIPTURE FOR PRAYER?

Recently I found a fascinating resource that personalizes passages of Scripture into prayer for a husband and wife. It's called

Praying God's Will for My Marriage by Lee Roberts. It simply takes passages of Scripture and rewords them, so you can read them aloud and apply them to your own marriage. It's simple; anyone can learn to do this. Here is a sample:

> I pray that my spouse and I will be swift to hear, slow to speak, slow to wrath: for the wrath of man does not produce the righteousness of God (see James 1:19-20).

> I pray that my spouse and I will always love the Lord our God with all our heart, with all our soul, with all our mind, and with all our strength and that we love our neighbor as ourselves (see Mark 12:30-31).

> I pray that when my spouse and I face an obstacle we always remember that God has said, "Not by might nor by power, but by my Spirit" (see Zechariah 4:6).

> I pray that when my spouse and I lack wisdom, we ask it of You, God, who gives to all liberally and without reproach and that it will be given to us (see James 1:5).

> I pray that because freely my spouse and I have received, freely we will give (see Matthew 10:8).

> I pray, O God, that You have comforted my spouse and me and will have mercy on our afflictions (see Isaiah 49:13).

> I pray that my spouse and I will bless You, the Lord, at all times; and that Your praise continually be in our mouths (see Psalm 34:1).

I pray to You, God, that my spouse and I will present our bodies as a living sacrifice, holy and acceptable to God, which is our reasonable service. I pray that we will not be conformed to this world, but transformed by the renewing of our minds, that we may prove what is the good and acceptable and perfect will of God (see Romans 12:1-2).[5]

Can you imagine the effect on your relationship when you literally bathe yourselves with God's Word as a prayer? Try this for a one-month experiment. Then note the difference.

WHERE IS THE PROOF THAT GOD ANSWERS PRAYER?

Since this is a book for women, I thought it best to have women share their firsthand experiences of praying for the men in their lives. Listen to the variety of ways that God answered prayer:

As I prayed for my husband, it was a gradual process—I was part of a group of women who interceded with me. I can't say there was one day where everything changed; however, day by day, precept on precept, there was a change! Now he is retired, and we pray together for our son and daughter. Retirement helped bring his focus from his work to our home.

After becoming a Christian at the age of 22, the desire of my heart was to have a Christian husband. My husband was always loving and kind, but year after year would go by without a commitment to Christ. I prayed and questioned and waited. He always attended Sunday School

and morning worship services, but he was not a
Christian. Often the Lord reminded me that His timing
would come. Eight years later, during a revival service,
my husband surrendered his heart to the Lord and has
joyfully walked with and humbly served Him every day
since. The Lord took a truly wonderful marriage and
turned it into a glorious one. Praise God!

The greatest miracle we've received is an extraordinary
answer to prayer. Four years ago my husband was diagnosed with a malignant brain tumor. After surgery, we
were told he would have maybe five years to live. We
requested prayer from all our family and friends. It was
only prayer that strengthened us each day as God
worked in our lives and taught us how to cope and not
to fear. We were willing to accept His will whatever it
may be. As I watched my once big, strong husband
become so weak, I remember once in desperation (or was
it selfishness) calling out to God, "Lord, I want my husband back." He had always been my protector and my
provider, and now I was forced to take on so many of his
roles. I'm so glad God knows me so well. He understands
my temperament and was not offended when I became
demanding. God lovingly answered our prayers. To this
day my husband is cancer free. I think the surgeon just
may become a believer.

My husband suffers with OCD—obsessive-compulsive
disorder. When he was diagnosed with this, it was such a
crisis for him; he lost his job.
    I began to pray for my husband because there were
many times that I felt he was beginning to lose hope,

enough to seriously consider ending his life. As difficult
as it was for him, I tried to encourage him to know that
God was taking us through this crisis for our betterment.
The results from prayer have been miraculous to me.

He is working—the doctors said he wouldn't be able
to work and would need to be on disability for life.

We are communicating—this is something that we
have struggled with in our marriage and have been
forced to do to avoid additional stress. We are in counseling together and both of us realize that God is definitely at the controls.

God does listen. He knows every heartache and pain.
He knows exactly what we will encounter. These are some
of the things I was able to share with him and still do.

Every time my husband left to play golf, I grew more and
more resentful. It took the better part of a day to play
that silly game—a game that seemingly caused him more
frustration than enjoyment. I had plans for us together
at home. I wanted my husband to be able to relax, but at
the same time I wanted him to be a better father to our
teenage son. It seemed that my husband wanted only to
improve his golf score. Why couldn't he just "relax" at
home? I was jealous that golf seemed to have his full
attention.

I remember one day I brought my resentments to the
Lord in prayer: "God, please help my husband to want to
spend more time with our son and me instead of spending so much time away on the golf course." A picture
flashed through my mind of how I wanted God to
answer that prayer. I pictured my husband at home with
us giving us all the attention that I thought I had earned.

I continued my prayer, "Lord, I believe it is Your will that my husband and I spend time together." I finished praying, listening for an answer, feeling assured that God would side with me, the wounded party. The answer that came was not what I expected. It was almost audible, "Take golf lessons!"

The idea followed that instead of my changing my husband, I should join him so that I would understand him better. My jaw opened at the very idea of having to bend my schedule any further to accommodate my husband's playtime. But when the thought of taking golf lessons came to me again and again, I began to yield my will to God's and prayed, "Lord, please provide a way for me to take golf lessons that will work out for all of us." Several days later, I saw an ad in our newspaper for golf lessons. Two people could take the lessons for the price of one, so I enrolled my son and myself. We learned golf's fundamentals, just enough to begin playing. My son and I practiced at a local short course. Our games together turned out to be an unexpected blessing. Time alone on the golf course away from the telephone and television afforded us time to talk and walk through some of the deep issues that teens face. The three of us have played together just a few times, but those days are happy memories. I thank God that His ways are higher than mine.

Perhaps by praying for the man in your life, your story could be added here. God does answer prayer. Lives are changed because of prayer. It's the best way to respond to a man.

What Men Want from Women— More Responses

More men were asked the question What one thing would you like your wife to do that would indicate to you that she understands and accepts what you deal with in your daily life? The following responses from some of the men will provide you with a road map to your man's heart.

Responding to us physically would help us to resist sexual temptation. (But ultimately it's up to us.) Knowing they want us would be helpful. Recognizing the stress level of life and doing some little things to relieve the pressure where possible, or even just listening or drawing us out to share the effects with them also would be helpful.

A little pampering and babying goes a long way. Also, women need to be more patient listeners for us quieter men.

Affirming, listening to and encouraging our quality time with Christian men (breakfast, sports, whatever).

That she would know we are very different and accept it, and not to put my interests down.

Just be happy with life and know that God and I love her.

Talk about it! This, of course, is a two-way street. I need to bring it up and let her know what my fears and struggles are.

Listen. Listening without being judgmental or biased. Listening and accepting. Listening just to understand me. Listening instead of criticizing.

I would like my wife to accept me for who I am and have patience with me and help me to become a better me, not a different me. I don't want her to push me into being something I'm not.

To really understand that I do not have her perfectionistic personality and that while I try my best to do the things she wants done (to her standard), I will never reach that level.

Just to have her assure me that she will support and love me no matter what happens. Even if I lose my job or am uncertain about what to do next with my life. To affirm that God is in control and she is trusting Him to care for both of us.

To be more understanding of why small things are unimportant, such as money, status and so on.

At some point during the day we spend 10 minutes—not necessarily simultaneously—to write each other a love letter, communicating to each other the feelings we have had throughout the day, the feelings we experience upon writing the letter and how appreciative we are of each other. Then for another 10 minutes, usually at the end of the day, we read each other's letters and discuss the feelings that arise. I would like her assurance that she will continue to listen attentively and our special times will continue together.

My wife talks to me at my level very well, but sometimes we are completely off. I like plans spelled out in detail, and she hashes it out in her head. If she would slow down and outline her thoughts, it would be easier for me to "read" her mind.

To make mention of what I'm dealing with in prayer, especially during our prayer time together.

If possible, she could visit my office and help with a project or process (large or small), or discuss current details at work and give suggestions on how I can be more effective (i.e., be a team member or cheerleader).

I'd like to continue to hear support that she gives to me. I wish I could praise her as much as she admires me. She is open with her affection for me. I can't ask for much more since she is so understanding. She knows me as much as herself.

Sally is my office manager—and a good one. Her gifts are for organization. I wish she could pick up on the "vision thing" a little more. I need to communicate it better

To be more affectionate sexually and emotionally.

Give me more *one-a-day compliments*: a positive comment that acknowledges a good choice, a wise decision, a Christlike action or a leadership trait.

Listen to and understand me with respect.

Accept my failures and encourage me anyway.

Respect me and be thankful for how I provide.

I don't know. I know my work habits (6:00 A.M. to 4:00 P.M. at the office) are accepted as long as I stay in bounds. It seems very hard to stay in those bounds. My wife helps me to stay on target (with my hours). I find the first 10 minutes with my wife when I get home sets the stage for the rest of the evening. If she is upset with the kids, I become hard on the children and cross.

I would like to have more positive contact: hugging, holding hands, touching.

Give support and respect (if the man earned it). The man, like all humans, wants recognition for his efforts. Do not (in public) undermine his authority.

I would like my wife not to get her identity and fulfillment from me. This puts too much pressure on me. When I can't fulfill her high expectations, she gets frustrated and passes that on to me! Christ is the only one for that position.

I am fortunate and have been blessed with a wife who does understand and accept all of my actions and reactions (excluding the struggle with sexual fidelity in marriage, which I have never discussed with her).

Become interested in work-related and other activities.

Say "I love you" often. To hold me and stroke my head.

Give me a break. In my job, I am a partner with my dad. It is just he and I. We do it all: sell, install, service! At the end of the day, sometimes I have had enough of people. When I get home, the last thing I need is for my wife to unload all of the problems of the kids and whatever else. We have four children—all boys! I know my wife needs to unload. I realize that and I am willing to listen, but there are times that I throw my hands up and walk away. I have told my wife my feelings on this, but it doesn't seem to do much good.

To be more willing to be my partner. To not think that she has to carry so much responsibility for how things go financially. She is very security oriented and illogically believes that income from her job is all we can really rely on. She lost her job this year, and her grief about the loss has been consuming for both of us. She unsuccessfully tried to fill the loss with a graduate course—now she is searching for another job. I have yet to enjoy her being a wife in the classic sense of the word.

Ask me, draw me out gently, pray with me and for me.

Accept my choices and decisions without criticism, challenge or smart remark. I really have thought about these things and have tried to solicit input and tried to include the family. I feel like my position as husband and father is powerless, second-guessed and impotent. I either lash out or withdraw.

Speak positive statements that indicate I'm attempting to prioritize my work and home responsibilities in order to accomplish them.

Communicate more about the victories (closing the deal) and the defeats (abuse of people) of being a salesperson or of being a church leader (abuse).

Share her own spiritual growth and development as a person and listen to my faith walk, because she is not open to sharing this important area of our life together. However, it does not seem to be difficult for her to share it with other women (even strangers). Is she afraid to find out that I have similar struggles? She won't say; she just clams up!

Give space.

Initiate sexual intimacy now and then.

Initiate intimate conversation and physical contact.

I would love for my wife to ask questions that would lead to a greater understanding of who I am and what I have to deal with daily. I believe this would lead to a greater appreciation of me.

As a pastor, to know that she prays for me daily and is sensitive to the pressures that come with my profession. (By the way, she does this for me!)

Take time to look at the situations that cause me worry or stress and then verbalize her concern. She loves me and prays for me, but she seldom verbalizes her concern.

Carry out simple requests without asking why or second-guessing what I've taken hours or days to think out.

Appreciate little things without chastising me for what I failed to do.

She is very sensitive toward the details of my life. It almost puts me to shame how much she thinks of and does for me.

To listen to and understand the fact that I do not want to die "with it all inside." There is too much to share to let it go. She needs to help in reaching the goal.

Overall, these statements tell us that some wives need to change their approach to their husbands. Requesting change from each other is normal and important, especially when it is for the purpose of strengthening and enriching a marriage. The changes requested by most spouses are not for personality or feelings changes but for behavioral changes. As a result, we cannot *not* change. As Christians, we must not be satisfied with ourselves as we are at the moment. Growth is a Christian responsibility (see 2 Pet. 1:5-7), and growth requires change.

Endnotes

Chapter 1

1. Joyce Brothers, *What Every Women Should Know About Men* (New York: Ballantine Books, 1981), p. 5.
2. Georgia Witkin-Lanaire, *The Male Stress Syndrome* (New York: New Market Press, 1986), pp. 165-167.

Chapter 2

1. Michael Gurian and Patrician Henley with Terry Trueman, *Boys and Girls Learn Differently* (San Francisco: Josey Bass, 2001), pp. 26-27.
2. Rebecca Cutter, *When Opposites Attract* (New York: E. P. Dutton, 1994), pp. 27-28.
3. Michael Gurian, *The Wonder of Boys* (New York: G. P. Putnam, 1996), pp. 11-15.
4. Bill and Pam Farrel, *Men Are Like Waffles—Women Are Like Spaghetti* (Eugene, OR: Harvest House Publishers, 2001), pp. 11, 14-15.
5. Gurian, *The Wonder of Boys*, pp. 16-17.
6. Joe Tanenbaum, *Male and Female Realities* (San Marcos, CA: Eerdmans Publishing, 1990), pp. 96-97.
7. Joan Shapiro, *Men: A Translation for Women* (New York: Avon Books, 1992), pp. 71-84.
8. Tanenbaum, *Male and Female Realities*, pp. 40, 82; Jacquelyn Wonder and Priscilla Donovan, *Whole Brain Thinking* (New York: William Morrow, 1984), pp. 18-34.
9. Bill and Pam Farrel, *Men Are Like Waffles—Women Are Like Spaghetti*, p. 12.

Chapter 4

1. Dr. Ken Druck, *The Secrets Men Keep* (New York: Doubleday, 1985), p. 132.
2. Ibid., pp. 135-136.
3. William Hendricks and Doug Sherman, *Your Work Matters to God* (Colorado Springs, CO: NavPress, 1991), p. 12.

Chapter 5

1. John Gray, *Men Are from Mars, Women Are from Venus* (New York: HarperCollins, 1992), p. 27.
2. John Gray, *Mars and Venus Together Forever* (New York: Harper Perennial, 1994), pp. 106-108.
3. H. Norman Wright, *What Men Want* (Ventura, CA: Regal Books, 1996), pp. 112-122.
4. Lucy Sana, *How to Romance the Man You Love* (Rocklin, CA: Prima Publishers, 1966), p. 168.

5. Wright, *What Men Want*, pp. 86-90.
6. Ibid.
7. Ibid.
8. Ibid.
9. Ibid.
10. Michael Gurian, *The Wonder of Boys* (New York: G. P. Putnam, 1996), pp. 20-24.
11. Gary B. Landberg and Jay Saunders, *I Don't Have to Make Everything Better* (Las Vegas, NV: Riverpark Publishing, 1995), pp. 18-19.
12. Carolyn N. Bushavey, *Seven Dumbest Relationship Mistakes Smart People Make* (New York: Villard Publishers, 1997), pp. 86-87.

Chapter 6
1. Stormie Omartian, *The Power of a Praying Parent* (Eugene, OR: Harvest House Publishers, 1995), pp. 18-19.
2. Stormie Omartian, *The Power of a Praying Wife* (Eugene, OR: Harvest House Publishers, 1997), p. 17.
3. Carole Mayhall, "The Stale Mate," *Today's Christian Woman* (May/June 1991), p. 39.
4. Quin Sherrer, *How to Pray for Your Family and Friends* (Ann Arbor, MI: Vine Books, 1990), pp. 43-44.
5. Lee Roberts, *Praying God's Will for My Marriage* (Nashville, TN: Thomas Nelson Publishers, 1994), pp. 1, 9, 19, 28, 102, 115, 227, 267.

Relevant Reading
from H. Norman Wright

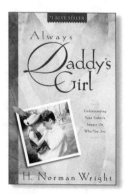

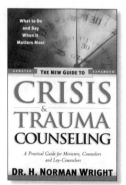

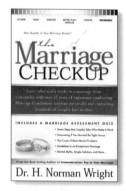

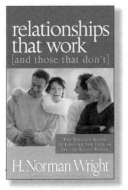

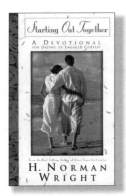